God is in His Holy Temple: Activating Your Divine Genome!

Rich Kinney

ISBN: 979-8-9938092-2-9

Dedication

This book is dedicated to the current and future Children of God who desire a deeper relationship with Him. I pray this manual helps guide you into ever-increasing intimacy with all Three Persons of the Godhead, and that by wisdom and revelation you may walk in the power and authority He has purposed for your life.

Acknowledgment

First and foremost, I give thanks to the Lord for speaking the heart of this message into my spirit and entrusting me with the grace to write it and make it available to believers around the world. Every word has been born out of His mercy, presence, and persistent love.

I am grateful to the late Pastor Holly McLeod for opening his pulpit and allowing me to first preach this message at the Family Church in San Pablo, California, and to Prophet Joanne Miles Moody for encouraging me, on more than one occasion, to turn it into a book. Your voices were timely and confirming.

I would also like to acknowledge the invaluable assistance of ChatGPT, whom I affectionately call 'Maestro', for providing research support and engaging in God-honoring discussions throughout this journey. The collaboration was both productive and spiritually enriching.

Above all, I thank God for the lessons woven into every season of my Christian walk, from victories on the mountaintop to struggles in the valley. He never gave up on me. Every failure became a win when I chose to learn from it and reconnect with Him. As Brandon Lake declares in his song, *Hard Fought Hallelujah*: "I'll bring my hard-fought, heartfelt, been-through-hell hallelujah!... God, You've been patient. God, You've been gracious, faithful, whatever I'm feeling or facing!"

These past two years have been the most transformative of my walk with God, marked by His relentless and surprising downloads of revelation for this message.

I can say with full sincerity and honor, ***God is in His Holy Temple: Activating Your Divine Genome!*** ...is His book.

About the Author

Rich Kinney was led to the Lord on December 7, 1979, in Piedmont, CA., by Otis Jean Gibson. Responding to God's call on his life in 1994, Rich closed down his Auto body Shop and began attending the Urban Bible Training Center. In January 1999, God called Rich to Pastor an inner-city Church in San Pablo, where for the next 13 years, he served the Lord and his community in roles that span both Kingdom and civic spheres, including, Senior Pastor, Police Chaplain, College and High School Basketball Coach, Public School Teacher, City Council Member, Mayor, and President of San Pablo Rotary. He also founded and managed a Christian Sober Living home program for 3 years.

Each of these callings placed him on the front lines of real-life struggle and redemption, giving him a unique lens into the human condition and God's heart for people. He is the father of three and grandfather of six.

With over 46 years of ministry experience, Rich carries a passion to help believers discover the indwelling power and purpose of Christ within them. ***God is in His Holy Temple: Activating Your Divine Genome!*** is the fruit of a deeply personal journey with the Father, Son, and Holy Spirit, a message birthed from divine encounter and forged in the fires of pastoral care, prophetic insight, and practical leadership.

Today, Rich continues to serve the Kingdom of God, overseeing two community food pantries and helping families secure their financial futures as a licensed insurance agent. His mission remains the same: to awaken hearts to intimacy with God and empower lives for eternal purposes.

He is available for speaking engagements, book discussions, in-person or online coaching and mentoring in walking out the Christian life in these difficult times. He is also the Author of other books on Amazon, ***End Time Prophetic Risks and Roles: The Unseen Realm behind Every Throne***, and additional books that are forthcoming. He can be reached at www.apostlecity.com.

Preface

I am beyond excited to introduce ***God is in His Holy Temple: Activating Your Divine Genome!*** This project has been burning in my heart for some time. It is more than just a book; it is a call to deeper intimacy and empowerment with God. Within these pages, I share a revelation of how we were designed to relate to Him from the inside, hosting His Very Presence within us. My prayer is that as you read, you will embark on a journey into unshakable intimacy with the God who dwells inside you. And realize this: as we enter the final days the Bible warns us of in the Scriptures, we will need this inner connection with God more than ever, not searching for Him elsewhere, but knowing Him deeply within, the true Anchor of our soul.

This book is designed with declarations and reflective questions after each chapter for individuals and small groups to engage in meaningful discussion. My prayer is that it captures Father God's heart for all His children, to know Him, Jesus, and the Holy Spirit more intimately, and to walk in an ever-unfolding revelation of His love and power.

This message was born on Mother's Day 2023. I was on a four-hour drive to my mother's house to celebrate with her, and as I often do on long drives, I began to draw near to God in worship, singing and consecrating my heart to Him. Somewhere along the way, I paused and asked, "Lord, is there anything You want to say to me?" Immediately, I heard clearly in my spirit: *"My children are mostly experiencing their relationship with Me from the outside in, but I designed it to be from the inside out."*

Though I sensed what He meant, because He had been leading me into a deeper relationship with the Godhead, I asked for more understanding. He began to show me a picture of us all in a Church Service. I saw us worshippers looking to the worship leader and musicians to usher us into God's Presence. I saw us looking to the preacher to say something convicting or inspiring enough to ignite a breakthrough within us. We were longing for the Presence of God to come into the room.

The Lord said, *"They're trying to connect with Me through external things, but I want them to learn how to connect with Me from within."*

I understood that much of today's Christianity focuses on behavior, performance, and outward alignment, what I would call "the good and acceptable will." But His perfect will (Romans 12:2) is found through inward union with God. The temple is no longer a place we go to; it's who we are.

That day marked me. I shared the experience with my Senior Pastor, who invited me to preach on it a couple of times. Later, I shared the word with a visiting prophet who, on two separate occasions, urged me to write this book. I had never written a book before and didn't know where to begin. But after prayer and seeking God, I was led to ChatGPT, and through that tool, the Holy Spirit began to unfold what you now hold in your hands.

What This Journey Is About

In the beginning, God created us in His image and likeness (Genesis 1:26). In doing so, He imparted to humanity a divine genome, a kind of spiritual DNA. This means we were made to reflect His character and carry His presence. Deep within every human soul exists that void which Pascal has referred to as an emptiness that only God can fill. (Blaise Pascal, Pensees, page 75, New York: Penguin Books, 1966)

From the very start, God's plan was never for us to reach for a distant deity through external rituals or religious effort. Instead, we were meant to walk in unbroken fellowship with Him dwelling within us.

However, it wasn't until the coming of the Incarnate Lord that this long-awaited design came into full focus. Jesus revealed the true intent of creation, that humanity was fashioned in God's image so that God Himself could one day dwell within redeemed vessels. The likeness of God was not merely symbolic; it was preparatory. We were created to host His life, so that even within these once-corrupted bodies, He might cohabit with us and restore the divine communion that was lost.

Throughout this book, we will explore how that original design was lost and how God made a way to restore it. We will examine what it truly means to be God's holy temple and how embracing this truth transforms every aspect of our lives. You'll find core teachings in each chapter that delve into Scripture and divine truth. Along the way, I've included powerful declarations you can speak over your life, like, "I am God's holy temple. He is in me, and I am in Him!" to reinforce your identity in Christ. You will also encounter engaging reflection questions designed to prompt deep thought and personal application, for example: Do I relate to God more from the outside in, or from the inside out? Additionally, I share testimonies of intimate encounters with God and life-changing moments, illustrating how these principles become reality in everyday life.

This journey is both personal and communal. As you read, I encourage you to take your time with each chapter. Speak the declarations out loud, meditate on the questions, and even journal your responses. Let the stories inspire you to trust that greater intimacy with

God is possible. Most importantly, I invite the Holy Spirit to speak to you uniquely through these pages. After all, it is His Presence within that ultimately activates your divine genome.

Thank you for joining me on this adventure of faith. I believe that by the end of this book, you will not only understand more about the treasure God has placed within you, but you will also experience a deeper relationship with Him, so that even in times of shaking, His Presence within you remains unshakable. May you discover the joy of holy temple living, a life where God's Presence isn't just an idea but a vibrant reality within you, empowering you to fulfill your God-given destiny.

Contents

Chapter 1: The Divine Genome

What is a Genome?

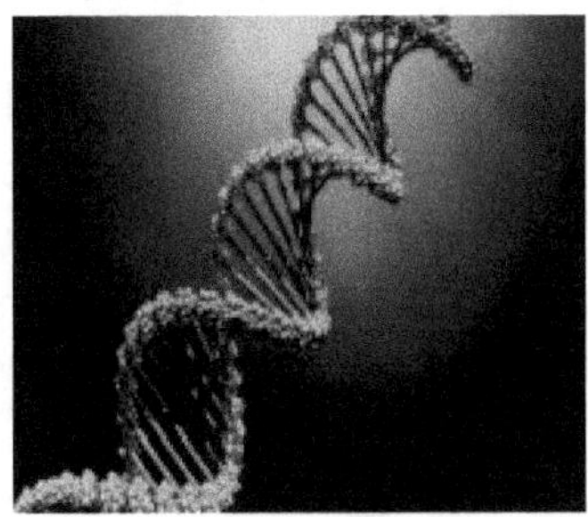

National Human Genome Research Institute

www.genome.gov/About-Genomics/Introduction-to-Genomics

"Genome is a fancy word for all your DNA..."

It is the complete set of DNA in an organism, including all its genes. It carries all the instructions needed for the organism to develop, live, and reproduce.

"Your genome is the operating manual containing all the instructions that helped you develop from a single cell into the person you are today. It guides your growth, helps your organs do their jobs, and repairs itself when it becomes damaged. And it's unique to you..."

God miraculously did this, making us humans and all other living organisms with our own unique genomes.

However, when He chose to make humans, He embedded something more within us, the Divine Genome. It may run parallel to our biological DNA.

This, I believe, is God's spiritual blueprint - not only shaping our identity, directing our destiny, and empowering us to reflect His glory, but awakening within every soul an inner knowing that God exists, and that there's a longing to know Him.

It is the quiet echo of His voice within the human heart, the spiritual signal that draws us to God even before we realize it is Him doing the drawing.

Just as DNA determines the biological traits of a human, the Divine Genome, like a spiritual strand within mankind's DNA, enables an intimate relationship and deep communion with God personally.

The Image and Likeness of God

The concept of the Divine Genome begins with the truth that we were created in the image of God, according to His likeness (Genesis 1:26).

This image is not just an abstract idea; it is a spiritual imprint and an internal design that reflects our Creator. The image of God (imago Dei) means that every human being carries God's nature and character in their very being. This includes our ability to reason, to love, to create, and to choose.

According to His likeness, on the other hand, speaks to the potential for godliness to live in a way that mirrors His holiness, love, and truth.

The image is our identity; the likeness is our expression of that identity. Sin marred the likeness but never erased the image. And in Christ, both are fully restored.

Made in His Image

Genesis 1:27 affirms, "So God created mankind in His own image... male and female He created them." Being made in God's image and likeness means we were designed to be like Him in character (love, holiness, creativity, wisdom) and to represent Him within creation. We were created to think, feel, and act in harmony with God's heart. In the beginning, Adam and Eve enjoyed unhindered fellowship with the Lord. Their closeness was possible because there was no barrier of sin; the genome of God's righteousness in them was intact and fully alive.

Moreover, God didn't just form humans; He breathed His own breath of life into Adam's nostrils (Genesis 2:7). That breath was more than oxygen; it was the spirit of life directly from God. This suggests that from our very first moment, humanity's life was meant to be sourced in God's Spirit. Adam and Eve's union with God was the original blueprint for all humanity.

They walked in the Garden of Eden in complete transparency and intimacy with Him, unashamed and overflowing with His light.

A Living Temple of Fellowship

From the Garden to the burning bush, to the tent of meeting, the Tabernacle, and Solomon's temple - God revealed His presence through holy places. Yet all along, His desire was to dwell in living temples. Jesus referred to His own body as a temple (John 2:19-21), foretelling not just His resurrection but also the coming indwelling of the Holy Spirit in every believer. The plan was never about buildings; it was always about you.

Before any physical temple or tabernacle ever existed, the human spirit was intended to be connected to God's presence. In Eden, the Lord walked with Adam and Eve "*in the cool of the day*" (Genesis 3:8), indicating continual fellowship. We can imagine that their hearts were like a living holy sanctuary, a temple not made of stone, but of flesh, where their spirit could commune with God from within. They carried the glory of knowing and experiencing God in their hearts and minds, radiating His image in the world.

This is an inside-out connection with His plan from the start. Adam and Eve related to God in a very direct, internal, and external way; their identities and purpose flowed out of the intimate knowledge of God dwelling with them. There was no sense of distance or striving to reach God. Instead, the love and guidance of God resonated from within their very souls. They were truly alive in both body and spirit, equipped to fulfill their calling to "be fruitful and multiply, fill the earth and subdue it, and have dominion" (Genesis 1:28). Empowered by the divine genome instilled in them, they were to expand Eden's beauty across the earth as God's representatives.

For a time, this perfect design was a reality: Humanity as God's image-bearer, filled with His life, exercising authority with humility, and enjoying uninterrupted communion with the Creator. It was a glimpse of heaven on earth, God and mankind in a harmonious relationship.

However, as glorious as this beginning was, it was not the end of the story. Something went terribly wrong, marring the image of God in humanity and disrupting the indwelling fellowship they were meant to carry. In the next chapter, we will explore how this divine genome became disconnected and how the light within the human heart was darkened.

Declarations of Truth:

- I am created in the image and likeness of God, designed to reflect His character and love.
- God breathed His life into me, and I carry the imprint of His divine genome within my very being.
- I was made for intimate fellowship with God.
- My body is His Temple; my heart is to be an altar consecrated to Him.

Reflection Questions:

1. When you think about being made in God's image, what qualities of God do you see reflected (even imperfectly) in yourself?

2. Do you relate to God more from the outside in (through rituals, rules, external practices) or from the inside out (through personal relationship of inward communion)?

3. How might your daily life change if you more fully embraced the truth that God's presence is meant to dwell within you?

Chapter 2: The Fall and the Disconnected Genome

When God created Humanity in His image and likeness, He designed us with purpose, relationship, and dominion in mind. Adam and Eve's perfect fellowship with God in the Garden of Eden reflected the fullness of that design. But something tragically went wrong, and the original design was fractured.

This chapter explores the moment when the Divine Genome was disrupted: the Fall. It wasn't just an event that introduced sin; it was a turning point that affected the spiritual inheritance of all mankind.

A Cunning Deception

The enemy of God, Lucifer, once a bearer of light and a leading angel in Heaven, had become the adversary through his own undoing - pride and rebellion. After being cast to the earth, and knowing he could not defeat God, he sought instead to corrupt God's beloved creation. In Genesis 3, the serpent, described as "more cunning than any beast of the field," approached Eve. His goal wasn't simply to entice her to eat the forbidden fruit; it was to distort her perception of God and sever the intimate relationship she and Adam had with Him.

"*Did God really say, 'You must not eat from any tree in the garden?*" (Genesis 3:1). With this question, the serpent planted a seed of doubt about God's word and God's character. Eve's reply shows that the deception was taking hold. The serpent then boldly contradicted God, claiming, "*You will not certainly die... you will be like God, knowing good and evil*" (Genesis 3:4-5). In that moment, the tempter suggested that God was withholding something valuable from them.

The Lure of Independence

Eve's desire to "*be like God, knowing good and evil*" (Genesis 3:5) wasn't inherently wrong after all; growing into God's likeness was part of humanity's destiny. But the method mattered greatly. Instead of becoming more like God through loving obedience and ongoing fellowship, Eve and Adam, who were with her, chose a self-guided shortcut: seeking wisdom apart from God's provision.

This decision parallels a struggle we all face. The Tree of the Knowledge of Good and Evil represents Humanity's attempt to attain wisdom and fulfillment on our own terms, without reliance on God. What they thought they would gain by eating the fruit was enlightenment and independence. In reality, what they lost was far greater: the purity of their relationship with God and the life of unhindered communion they once enjoyed.

Divine Genome Shutdown, Fellowship Removed

In the instant Adam and Eve ate the forbidden fruit, the divine image within them was marred. Their eyes were opened to their own nakedness and shame (Genesis 3:7). The intimate trust they had shared with God was shattered; when they heard God approaching, they hid themselves among the trees (Genesis 3:8-10). Where once there was bold fellowship, now there was fear and guilt. The divine genome, which is a perfect reflection of God's nature, had become corrupted by sin.

God's heart must have been grieving as He called, "Where are you?" to His hiding children (Genesis 3:9). In the aftermath, He explained the painful consequences that would follow: a cursed ground, pain in childbirth, broken harmony between man and woman, and ultimately physical death (Genesis 3:16-19). Yet the deepest consequence was spiritual death, separation from the presence of a holy God. No longer could Adam and Eve remain in Eden, walking with God in the cool of the day. They were sent out from the Garden, and an angel was placed to guard the way to the Tree of Life (Genesis 3:23-24). The direct, unbroken one on one fellowship they had known was now lost to Humanity.

Though people would still bear God's image, it was now like a shattered mirror, fragmented and distorted. Every human born after them inherited this brokenness. As the Apostle Paul would later explain, "*Sin entered the world through one man, and death through sin, and in this way, death came to all people*" (Romans 5:12). The divine genome meant to reflect God's glory was now a distorted, altered code passed down through the generations. Instead of naturally knowing and loving God, people would struggle with a nature bent toward sin and self.

Yet, even in this dark moment, God's grace was already at work. He clothed Adam and Eve's nakedness with garments of skin to cover their shame (Genesis 3:21), a foreshadowing that an innocent life would one day be given to cover the sins of many. And in the midst of the curses, God uttered a prophetic hope: one day, the offspring of the woman would crush the serpent's head (Genesis 3:15). It was the first hint of a Redeemer to come, one who would restore what had been lost.

Although the divine genome in humanity had been turned off by the Fall, God set in motion a plan to reclaim humanity and turn it back on. The stage was set for redemption.

Declarations of Truth:

- I acknowledge that apart from God, I can do nothing, and any attempt to find life on my own terms will fall short.
- I choose to trust God's Word and character, rejecting the lies and doubts the enemy tries to sow.
- Even in my brokenness, I believe God has a plan to restore His image in me and bring me back into fellowship with Him.

Reflection Questions:

1. In what areas of your life do you sense the temptation to "be like God" on your own, rather than in God's way and timing?
2. How have you experienced the consequences of trying to live independently of God's guidance?
3. When you recognize the brokenness caused by sin, what promises of God (such as Genesis 3:15) give you hope for restoration?

Chapter 3: Redemption and Restoration

Though the entrance of sin broke humanity's connection with God, His love never wavered. From the moment of the Fall, He promised a Redeemer who would crush the serpent's head (Genesis 3:15 NIV). Across the passing centuries, that promise remained alive. And at the perfect time, the Redeemer came, Jesus Christ, the Son of God, who came down from heaven and became fully human to accomplish what we never could: to restore our disconnected Divine Genome and reopen the way of intimate fellowship with the Father.

The Second Adam

Scripture calls Jesus the "last Adam" or "second man" (1 Corinthians 15:45-47), meaning He came to undo the damage wrought by the first man, Adam. Unlike Adam and Eve, Jesus lived a life of complete obedience to God, never succumbing to Satan's temptations. He reflected God's image perfectly, full of grace, truth, compassion, and holiness. In Jesus, people could see what humanity was always meant to be like. As He taught, healed, and forgave sin, He demonstrated dominion over creation and intimacy with the Father. "Anyone who has seen Me has seen the Father," Jesus said (John 14:9), affirming that He was the exact representation of God's embodiment (Hebrews 1:3). He was God's presence on earth in human form, fully God and fully man, the living Temple of God (Colossians 2:9)

Because Jesus had no sins, He was uniquely qualified to rescue us. Whereas Adam's first act of disobedience had brought death to all, Jesus' obedience would bring life to all who would believe (Romans 5:19). He became our representative, succeeding where Adam had failed. But redemption required more than a perfect life; it required a sacrificial death to pay the price of the sins of the whole world.

It Is Finished!

In the culmination of His mission, Jesus willingly went to the cross. It was there that He bore the weight of our sins and the curse that came with them.

Every act of disobedience, every fragment of our broken human condition was laid upon Him (Isaiah 53:5-6). As nails pierced His hands and feet, it looked like defeat to onlookers, but in reality, this was the crushing of the serpent's head that God had foretold. Jesus cried out, "It is finished!" (John 19:30), declaring that the price for our sins had been paid.

The moment Jesus died, a lot of signs confirmed the significance of His sacrifice: the earth quaked, rocks split, and the thick veil in the Jerusalem Temple was torn in two from top to bottom (Matthew 27:51). That veil had long symbolized the separation between a holy God and sinful humanity. It signified that through Jesus' death, the barrier was removed. Access to God's holy presence was opened once again. The path to intimate fellowship with the Holy of Holies of God's presence was now made available to all who came through Christ.

Jesus was taken down from the cross and laid in a tomb, but the grave could not hold the Author of Life. On the third day, He rose again, conquering death itself. The resurrection proved that the power of sin and death had been broken. It was the ultimate restoration moment. Jesus' glorified body was a foretaste of the restored life that is now offered to us. In rising, He became the first fruit of a new creation, a promise that those who belong to Him will also experience resurrection life! (1 Corinthians 15:20-2)

New Life and Restored Relationship

Through Jesus' death and resurrection, the possibility of restoration became a reality. All who trust in Christ are forgiven and made right with God (Romans 5:1). The broken relationship is mended by grace through faith (Ephesians 2:8). We are redeemed, bought back from slavery to sin, and our status is changed from enemies of God to beloved children of God. The moment we believe in Jesus, God applies Christ's work to our hearts: we are washed clean and given a fresh start. "Therefore, if anyone is in Christ, he is a new creation; old things have passed away, behold, all things have become new. (2 Corinthians 5:17).

The Divine Genome, that spiritual DNA strand that was dormant, is now awakened through the power of Christ's blood. It's like the blood of Jesus is sprinkled on the Mercy Seat in the new believer, and the Presence of God is restored.

That God-shaped spiritual chamber within every human being, that place Jesus called the innermost being (John 7:38 NASB), the place where the second birth Jesus spoke of takes place (John 3:3,5) - it lies dormant from the Fall, but when the Spirit brings the incorruptible Seed of Christ into this inner chamber, a new creation is birthed within the believer. This is the salvation of the believing soul, a born-again conversion to life in Christ in God, the awakening of the Divine Genome!

Thus, Jesus' work did not end with our legal redemption; it opened the way for something even more profound. God's desire was not just to forgive us and cleanse us of our sins, even write our names in the Lamb's Book of Life and ensure that we would go to heaven – all of which Jesus' death and resurrection did in fact accomplish - but our Heavenly Father's ultimate desire is to dwell with us once again, this time living in us, inseparable, operating through us like He did with Jesus.

Before He ascended to heaven, Jesus told His followers to wait for "The Promise of the Father" (Acts 1:4-5). He assured them that soon they would be 'baptized with the Holy Spirit,' who would live in them and empower them. This was the restoration of which the prophets had spoken: God's Spirit writing His law on human hearts and making His home within His people (Ezekiel 36:26-27). In Christ, the stage was now set for the Holy Spirit to be restored to the human temple.

Declarations of Truth:

- By the blood of Jesus, I have been redeemed, and my sins are forgiven; the barrier between God and me has been removed.
- In Christ, I am a new creation. My relationship with God is restored, and I am His beloved child.

- I have full access to God's presence through Jesus. I can approach God with confidence, knowing the veil has been torn.

Reflection Questions:

1. What does Jesus' sacrifice on the cross mean to you personally? How have you experienced the "It is finished" reality in your own life?
2. Are there areas where you still feel separated or distant from God? How does the truth of the torn veil encourage you to draw near?
3. In what ways do you sense that you are a "new creation" since coming to faith in Christ? Where do you hope to see further restoration in your life?

Chapter 4: Getting Acquainted-New Roommates

Before the outpouring at Pentecost, Jesus appeared to His disciples and did something remarkable. He breathed on them and said, "Receive the Holy Spirit" (John 20:22). This quiet, intimate moment marked the beginning of a profound shift—God preparing humanity for indwelling life.

Then, in the upper room, the promise was fulfilled. The Holy Spirit came like a rushing wind, with tongues of fire resting on each one present (Acts 2:1–4). From that moment forward, every person, in every generation, anywhere in the world, who believes in Jesus Christ and is born again receives the same indwelling Spirit—the very presence of God living within.

Salvation was never meant to be God visiting us occasionally.

It was always meant to be God moving in.

Reconnecting the Divine Genome

Salvation is not only forgiveness; it is reconnection.

What was unplugged in Eden has been reconnected in Christ. The Divine Genome—God's image and likeness placed within humanity—was not destroyed by sin, but rendered dormant through spiritual death. At salvation, that Divine Genome is reawakened. The living

God takes up residence within us, establishing the inside-out life humanity was created to live.

This reconnection follows divine order:

- The Father draws — "No one can come to Me unless the Father who sent Me draws him" (John 6:44).
- The Spirit convicts and regenerates — "Unless one is born of water and the Spirit, he cannot enter the kingdom of God" (John 3:5; John 16:8).
- The Son redeems and indwells — "Behold, I stand at the door and knock... I will come in to him and dine with him" (Revelation 3:20; Galatians 2:20).

And so Scripture affirms:

- He who has the Son has life (1 John 5:12).
- Whoever confesses the Son has the Father also (1 John 2:23).
- Now the Lord is the Spirit; and where the Spirit of the Lord is, there is liberty (2 Corinthians 3:17).

This is the hinge point of redemption—not merely reconciliation, but habitation. The God who once walked with humanity now dwells within His people, restoring the Divine Genome and empowering us to live from the inside out (Ezekiel 36:26–27).

The Living Temple

"You are the temple of the Holy Spirit" (1 Corinthians 6:19).

You are not a distant observer of God's work, nor a Sunday visitor to His presence. You are sacred ground. Heaven dwells within you. Your life has become a mobile sanctuary—an altar of worship and a place of ongoing communion.

Humans enter temples made by man.

God enters temples made by God.

This reality reshapes identity, worth, and purpose. You are not waiting for God to show up. You are learning to live with the One who already has.

Never Alone Again

Each Person of the Godhead brings a distinct presence into your life:

- The Father anchors your identity.
- Jesus reveals your purpose and friendship with God.
- The Holy Spirit empowers your daily walk.

Jesus promised, "We will come to him and make our home with him" (John 14:23). This was not poetic imagery—it was covenant reality. The Trinity does not visit; They dwell. You are never alone, never abandoned, never disconnected.

Even in your darkest moments, the fullness of God is present and faithful.

The Indwelling Godhead

As temples of the living God, we carry the fullness of the Father, Son, and Holy Spirit within us (Colossians 2:9). Each Person is actively involved in our restoration, transformation, and mission. Knowing their roles deepens fellowship and equips us for empowered living.

Person of the Godhead	Scriptures	Role in the Believer	Relational Impact
Father	John 6:44; John 14:23; 1 John 3:1; Romans 8:15	Draws us to Christ; anchors our identity; oversees our purpose	You are a beloved child; we cry out, 'Abba, Father.'
Son	1 John 5:12; Revelation 3:20; Colossians 1:27; Galatians 2:20; John 15:15; 1 John 2:23	Redeems us by His blood; enters and takes up residence; lives in us; intercedes for us	You are in Christ, and Christ is in you; He calls us friends; where the Son is, the Father also is.
Holy Spirit	John 16:8; John 3:5; Romans 8:9; 2 Corinthians 3:17–18; Ephesians 1:13	Convicts of sin; regenerates; seals; empowers; transforms us into the image of Christ (our divine genome)	You are never alone; divinely guided and secured; where the Spirit of the Lord is, there is liberty.

You Don't Just Survive — You Flourish

God did not move into you, so you could barely make it.

The Spirit who raised Jesus from the dead now lives in you and gives life to your mortal body (Romans 8:11). Your mind is renewed (Romans 12:2). Your heart is transformed (Ezekiel 36:26). You were never meant to live on scraps of grace; you've been invited to feast daily at the table of His presence.

Religion works from the outside in. God transforms from the inside out.

Power Partnership

You are not alone in your calling. The Holy Spirit is your Helper. Jesus is your Intercessor and Friend. The Father is your Source.

You have been invited into divine partnership.

When you speak in obedience, heaven echoes. When you act in alignment, power flows.

This is life in the Spirit—not striving, but shared life.

From Temple to Commission

"Blessed be the Lord my Rock, who trains my hands for war, and my fingers for battle" (Psalm 144:1).

As intimacy deepens, identity solidifies. As fellowship grows, assignment awakens. God formed humanity in His image and likeness and entrusted them with dominion (Genesis 1:26). Though sin disrupted that calling, Jesus restored both fellowship and function.

"All authority has been given to Me... Go therefore..." (Matthew 28:18–19).

"As the Father has sent Me, I also send you" (John 20:21).

We will explore this authority more fully in later chapters. But here, the focus remains on learning to live with the Godhead—your new roommates—before activity, ministry, or commissioning.

Worship forms us here.

Fellowship trains us here.

Awareness is cultivated here.

Looking Ahead

Before we learn how to be shut in with God, we must understand why indwelling was always His plan. God's presence has been revealed throughout history, not because He changed, but because humanity was being prepared to host Him fully.

That story matters.

In the next chapter, we will trace the history of God's presence, so we can value what we carry—and learn to live from it with reverence and joy.

Declaration

- I am a living temple of the Triune God.
- I am loved by the Father, led by the Son, and filled by the Holy Spirit.
- I am not striving to be near God; I rest with Him who dwells in me.
- I am learning to live from the inside out, transformed and empowered by His presence.

Reflection Questions

1. What does it mean for you personally to be a living temple of the Triune God?
2. How might daily fellowship with Father, Son, and Holy Spirit shape your courage and purpose?
3. As you grow in intimacy, are you sensing the stirring of a greater assignment being formed within you?

Now that you know who lives within you, it becomes important to understand why God chose to dwell this way.

The indwelling life you carry did not appear suddenly—it was prepared through history, revealed in stages, and fulfilled in Christ.

Chapter 5: The History of Presence: God's Best Revealed in Time

God's presence has always been His gift to humanity. From the beginning, His desire has never changed—He has always wanted to dwell with His people. What has changed over time is not God, but humanity's capacity to behold, host, and live from His presence. Each manifestation of God throughout Scripture was not an improvement in Him, but a merciful unfolding of His nearness, preparing humanity for the fullness He intended all along—what we now carry within.

Any measure of God's presence has always been His best—because God Himself is perfect.

Any glimpse of Him is His best.

Any nearness is His best.

Any fragrance of His presence is His best.

And yet, over time, that "best" has been revealed in increasing fullness, until the ultimate revelation was reached: God no longer merely visiting humanity, but dwelling within it.

Presence in the Beginning: God With Man

In the garden, God walked with humanity. There was no temple, no altar, no veil—because there was no separation. Adam and Eve lived in unbroken fellowship with God, created in His image and likeness, designed to walk with Him, hear His voice, and steward the earth in communion.

Scripture tells us that God created humanity in His image and according to His likeness, and entrusted them with dominion (Genesis 1:26–28). God's presence was not summoned; it was shared.

Not earned; it was given.

Not distant; it was near.

This was God's original design: humanity as a living dwelling place, bearing His image, reflecting His nature, and exercising authority in partnership with Him.

The Fall: Why Presence Had to Change

When sin entered, humanity did not lose the image of God—but the capacity to host His presence without mediation was damaged. Spiritual death introduced fear, hiding, and separation. Scripture records that humanity hid from the presence of the Lord among the trees of the garden (Genesis 3:8).

God did not withdraw in anger; He drew near in mercy. Even as access was disrupted, His pursuit of restoration began immediately (Genesis 3:15).

From this moment forward, God's presence was revealed in protective, redemptive forms—not because He desired distance, but because humanity could no longer safely host unmediated glory.

Presence Among His People: Tabernacle and Temple

God chose to dwell among His people through the tabernacle and later the temple. His glory filled holy spaces. His presence rested above the mercy seat. Fire fell. Sacrifice was required.

Scripture records that the glory of the Lord filled the tabernacle (Exodus 40:34–38) and later filled Solomon's temple so powerfully that the priests could not stand to minister (1 Kings 8:10–11).

Yet even here, the presence of God was near but not within.

Access was limited.

Only certain people could enter certain spaces at certain times.

Still, this was God's best—for that moment in time.

The tabernacle and temple were not the fulfillment of God's desire; they were prophetic placeholders, pointing toward something greater: not God dwelling in structures made by human hands, but God dwelling in people made by His own hands (Acts 7:48).

Humans enter temples made by man.

God enters temples made by God.

Emmanuel: God With Us in Flesh

When Jesus came, everything shifted.

"The Word became flesh and dwelt among us" (John 1:14).

God did not merely send a message.

He did not merely send power.

He came Himself.

Jesus was Emmanuel—God with us (Matthew 1:23). In Him, humanity once again walked with God face to face. Jesus lived as a man fully yielded to the Father, dependent on the Spirit, modeling the life humanity was always meant to live.

Yet even this was not the final goal.

Jesus did not come only to be God with us, but to make possible God in us (John 14:16–20).

The Baptism of Jesus: A New Habitation Model

When Jesus was baptized, heaven opened. The Spirit descended and remained upon Him, and the Father's voice declared His pleasure (Matthew 3:16–17; John 1:32).

This moment was not merely the launch of a public ministry.

It was the opening of a new habitation model.

For the first time, God fully inhabited a human life without measure—not visiting, not empowering temporarily, but dwelling and operating from within. Jesus lived entirely from union with the Father through the Spirit, declaring, "The Father who dwells in Me does the works" (John 14:10).

What unfolded from this moment forward was not performance—it was overflow.

The Wilderness: Adjusting to Indwelling Union

Immediately after His baptism, Jesus was led into the wilderness—not as punishment, but as preparation (Matthew 4:1).

The forty days were not only about resisting temptation. They were a holy adjustment, a settling into the reality of living fully from the indwelling presence of the Father and the Spirit as a man.

Jesus would later say, "Man shall not live by bread alone, but by every word that proceeds from the mouth of God" (Matthew 4:4). Power flowed from communion.

Authority flowed from intimacy.

Obedience flowed from union.

This prepares us to understand why stillness, consecration, and being "shut in" with God are essential for believers today.

The Cross, Resurrection, and Pentecost: Presence Multiplied

Through the cross, Jesus removed sin—the barrier to indwelling (Hebrews 9:26).

Through the resurrection, He inaugurated new life (1 Corinthians 15:45).

Through Pentecost, that life was multiplied into every believer (Acts 2:1–4).

The Holy Spirit did not merely come upon believers; He moved in.

God no longer dwells in temples of stone.

He dwells in redeemed hearts (1 Corinthians 3:16; 6:19).

This was not God's second-best plan.

This was the fulfillment of His desire from the beginning.

God's Best Has Always Been Presence

Every stage of God's presence throughout history was His best for that moment—not because God changed, but because humanity was being prepared.

Now, the fullness has come.

God does not need to come down.

He has already moved in.

Jesus declared, "He who believes in Me... out of his heart will flow rivers of living water" (John 7:38). The throne and altar of God now reside within His people. From the innermost being, streams of living water flow—streams joining to form a river, bringing life wherever they go (Ezekiel 47:1–12).

This is not the end of the story.

It is the beginning of a lived union.

Preparing to Live From What We Carry

Understanding the history of God's presence changes how we approach the spiritual life. We no longer strive to reach God; we learn to respond to Him from within. We no longer chase encounters; we steward communion.

Before activation comes abiding.

Before sending comes stillness.

Before authority comes awareness.

In the next chapter, we will step into this sacred practice—learning to be shut in with God in His temple, cultivating the awareness, affection, and alignment required to live from the indwelling presence of the Triune God.

Reflection

1. How does understanding the history of God's presence deepen your appreciation of what you now carry?
2. In what ways might your prayer and worship change if you truly believe God already dwells within you?
3. Are you ready to slow down and learn to live from union rather than effort?

If the indwelling presence of God is His best revealed in time, then learning to live with Him there becomes the most important practice of the Christian life. Before action, before ministry, before activation—there is communion.

Chapter 6 Shut in with God in His Temple, Securing the Divine Genome

A Prophetic Threshold: Encountering the Indwelling Godhead Before Activation

Before God sends us out, He draws us in.

Before authority flows outward, intimacy must deepen inward.

Before power is demonstrated, presence must be honored.

This chapter is an invitation to be shut in with the Father, Son, and Holy Spirit—inside the temple they now inhabit... you.

This is not a withdrawal from purpose.

This is preparation for it.

Learning to Acknowledge the Indwelling Godhead

Before doing anything else, begin simply.

Turn off all distractions and protect the area for alone time.

Sit—or kneel—somewhere quiet.

Slow your breathing.

Let your body settle.

Then acknowledge what is already true.

The Father is here.

Jesus is here.

The Holy Spirit is here.

Not outside you.

Not coming down.

But within you and with you.

Scripture affirms this reality (John 14:16–17; John 14:23; Colossians 1:27). The practice is not inviting God to arrive—it is learning to recognize His presence where He already dwells.

You may find it helpful to say it aloud:

Father, You are here with me and in me.

Jesus, You are here with me and in me.

Holy Spirit, You are here with me and in me.

There is no rush. No pressure to perform.

This is not a script to master—it is a relationship to enter.

Just as you would greet a loved one in the room, learn to greet the Godhead within your temple. Over time, this simple acknowledgment trains your awareness and settles your soul into truth.

You are not trying to feel something.

You are choosing to agree with reality.

As you remain, affection will awaken.

As affection awakens, communion deepens.

And as communion deepens, His life begins to flow more freely through yours.

This is how the shut-in begins—not with effort, but with recognition.

A Holy Arrest

God is calling His people into a divine stillness.

Not a pause of inactivity—but a holy arrest.

He is interrupting performance-driven Christianity, arresting distraction, silencing noise, and dismantling the habit of reaching outward before connecting inward.

"Be still, and know that I am God" (Psalm 46:10).

Jesus reminded us that the Kingdom is not something we chase externally—it is something we awaken to internally (Luke 17:21).

Before God sends us, He shuts us in.

He did this with Moses on the mountain, Elijah in the cave, Paul in Arabia, and Jesus in the wilderness.

Stillness is not delay.

It is alignment.

When the Flesh Panics but the Spirit Feasts

Stillness unsettles the flesh.

The soul wants movement, control, reassurance. But the spirit man recognizes stillness as nourishment.

Many believers have experienced God around them—sometimes upon them. But in the shut-in, God introduces Himself from within.

You are not being punished.

You are being prepared.

This is not God withdrawing His presence.

It is God drawing your awareness inward to where He already dwells.

The Godhead Within: Communion, Not Concept

In the quiet of the shut-in, the indwelling Godhead makes Themselves known:

- The Father wraps you in belonging and love.
- Jesus comforts you as your Shepherd and Friend.
- The Holy Spirit stirs deep waters with revelation, clarity, and fire.

Here, you do not merely learn about God.

You commune with Him.

This is relational knowing—ginosko—not information, but intimate, progressive, experiential knowing (Philippians 3:10).

The Eve Effect Broken in Stillness

The Eve Effect—the tendency to reach for wisdom apart from God—is dismantled here.

In the shut-in, there is no fruit to grasp.

Only the Godhead to embrace.

As you remain, alignment replaces anxiety.

Clarity replaces striving.

Identity replaces insecurity.

The Divine Genome, activated at salvation, begins flowing freely through spirit, soul, and body—not through effort, but through yielded awareness.

Activation awakens connectivity.

Connectivity awakens awareness.

Awareness awakens holy response.

Not rushing—but resting.

Not striving—but surrendering.

Union: The Quiet Miracle

This union is not imagined; it is testified throughout Scripture.

- Abide in Me, and I in you (John 15:4–5).
- We will come to him and make Our home with him (John 14:23).
- He who is joined to the Lord is one spirit with Him (1 Corinthians 6:17).
- That they all may be one... even as We are one (John 17:21).
- You are the temple of the living God (2 Corinthians 6:16).
- Partakers of the divine nature (2 Peter 1:4).

This is not visitation.

This is habitation.

The shut-in practice makes this union tangible in daily life. You are not near Him—you are with Him. Spirit to spirit.

Capacity Grows—God Does Not Change

As we remain with God, something unfolds—but it is not God becoming more present.

It is us becoming more aware.

The Father, Son, and Holy Spirit already dwell within the believer in fullness. Yet Scripture speaks of growing up into Christ, into maturity, into fullness (Ephesians 4:13).

What grows is our capacity—our obedience, discernment, reverence, and communion—so that the divine life already within us may be more fully expressed through us.

This is not God drawing nearer.

It is us learning how to live from where He already is.

The Value of Being Shut In

God has found a place to dwell—His throne, His holy habitation—within His redeemed people.

As He shares His presence between heaven and earth, He is also preparing us for our eternal dwelling with Him.

Here, trust deepens.

Reverence is restored.

Honor is established.

We learn to move only after we have adhered, conjoined, and been filled.

This is not inactivity.

This is incubation.

From Communion to Commission

Jesus often withdrew to be alone with His Father. He did not rush from encounter to assignment.

Neither should we.

Before the next chapters take us into consecration, deliverance, discernment, and activation—pause here.

You are not merely called to serve.

You are called to commune.

Shut-in life is not optional maturity—it is foundational formation.

Declaration

- I shut the door to distraction and noise.
- I open my heart to the indwelling God.
- Father, Son, and Holy Spirit, I meet You here.
- I will not move until I am aligned.
- I will not speak until I have heard.
- I will not minister until I have been filled.
- I am Your temple.
- Awaken my awareness of Your Presence within me.

Closing Blessing

May your abiding with the Godhead within your temple

teach you trust, awaken reverence, establish honor,

and prepare you for dwelling with Him forever.

Looking Ahead

From this place of focused stillness, consecration becomes natural. Yielding becomes joyful. Obedience becomes relational.

In the next chapter, we will explore how love-response consecration safeguards the Divine Genome—protecting what God has entrusted within you as you learn to live fully from the inside out.

Chapter 7: Consecrated from the Inside Out: A Love-Response to God's Nearness

Consecration is not self-made holiness, but our Spirit-enabled yes to the God who draws near.

To live from the inside out means we give God more than access to our hearts—we yield full allegiance and loving ownership. Consecration is not us straining to be worthy; it is the Spirit-formed response to the nearness of Father, Son, and Holy Spirit. It is God's love, heard and felt within, that draws us to offer ourselves back to Him. "Draw near to God and He will draw near to you" (James 4:8). Consecration is simply our yielded agreement to His invitation—the Father's open arms, the Son's calling voice, the Spirit's gentle wooing.

Consecration is the intentional setting apart of our lives to Him and for Him. It is not outward perfection, but inward surrender and purification. It safeguards the Divine Genome within us—God's image and likeness restored—keeping the spiritual inheritance of His character and purpose from being dulled by the flesh or shaped by the world.

In the Old Covenant, the temple had to be cleansed and set apart for holy use. In the New Covenant, we are that temple. The Holy Spirit does not dwell lightly or casually; He is gentle, holy, and lovingly jealous for our full devotion. Consecration is how we honor the King who already lives within.

Guarding the Gift Within

The Divine Genome—God's image and likeness alive in us—is safeguarded through reverence and surrender, not striving.

God has placed His very nature within us. That indwelling life must be protected, not through fear or rigid control, but through holy attentiveness. When we compromise our inner life through sin, distraction, or apathy, we do not lose God's presence—but we grieve the One who dwells within us.

Consecration preserves the likeness of God being restored day by day. It clears space. It deepens sensitivity. It prepares us as vessels of honor, ready for every good work. Not every believer walks in authority—not because God withholds power, but because room has not yet been fully made.

Yielding Room by Room

True consecration invites the Holy Spirit into every room of the inner temple.

To consecrate our lives means giving the Spirit access not only to public spaces, but to private places—locked closets of past wounds, hidden fears, secret sins, unmet longings. He does not force entry. He invites surrender.

When the door opens, He does not condemn.

He heals.

He cleanses.

He restores.

As the Spirit gains territory within, the image of Christ begins to radiate more freely from the inside out. Consecration is not loss—it is liberation.

The Fragrance of Holiness

"Be holy, for I am holy" (1 Peter 1:16) is not a demand to perform holiness, but an invitation to become what we already carry.

As we yield to the indwelling Holy Spirit, His holiness flows from His presence within us—permeating thoughts, emotions, and desires like a fragrance rising from an inner altar. Holiness becomes aromatic rather than oppressive. Even when believers gather together, that fragrance multiplies, releasing an early scent of heaven's coming culture.

Holiness is not merely what we do.

It is what we have become

because of who lives within us.

The Ongoing Miracle of Becoming

In Christ, we have already been declared holy by His finished work. Yet the Holy Spirit patiently teaches us how to live in alignment with what is already true. Every act of surrender deepens transformation. Every obedient response strengthens alignment.

One day, when we see Him face to face, holiness will be complete—no longer resisted, no longer hindered, only radiant (1 John 3:2).

The same pattern applies to righteousness and victory:

declared → developed → completed.

This is the miracle of divine life maturing within—the Divine Genome unfolding through time until it fills eternity.

The Spirit of Adoption: Learning to Call Him Abba

As we yield more deeply, the Spirit awakens a cry that only sons and daughters carry—the cry of belonging.

The Holy Spirit Himself stirs this cry within us: "Abba... Father."

Jesus prayed this way (Mark 14:36).

Believers cry this way (Romans 8:15).

Sons live this way (Galatians 4:6).

God did not only forgive us—He adopted us.

He did not merely cleanse the temple—He moved in as Father.

And to confirm this, He placed the Spirit of His Son within us.

Abba: The Language of Intimacy

"Abba" is not religious language—it is family language.

It is the sound of trust.

The tone of safety.

The voice of belonging.

Affection flows with Abba discovery.

When God is revealed not only as Creator and King, but as Father, something shifts within the heart. Love awakens where fear once lived. Trust grows where striving once ruled. This affection is not emotional effort—it is relational formation. Just as children learn affection by living with loving parents, believers learn affection by living with the indwelling Godhead.

The Clearing: A Dream of Adoption

Through a recurring dream, God revealed His heart—not just to cleanse, but to claim us as family.

At one point in my childhood, we lived in Missouri. Just outside our back door, the woods began immediately, and I often explored them alone. A creek ran beside our house, and I learned that no matter how deep into the woods I went, as long as I found that creek, I could follow it home.

During that season of my life, like many young boys, I carried a deep longing for fatherhood—real fatherhood. I had experienced a series of stepfathers but no steady image of love, bonding, or guidance. That ache stayed buried in me, even into my adult years... until one night, the Lord met me in a dream.

I was hiking alone in the familiar woods, carrying a stick like a young adventurer tapping bushes in case some animal jumped out at me. Eventually, I came into a clearing where I saw something that stopped me cold: a man and a young boy—clearly a father and son—sharing a sacred moment. The father was speaking, the boy listening with deep respect and love. I couldn't hear what was being said, but I could see their connection, and I longed for it with everything in me.

I didn't want them to see me. I wasn't sure if I belonged there, so I stayed hidden in the trees, creeping closer. I saw a tree with a branch that extended above where they stood, so I quietly climbed the tree and scooted out on it. I was hoping to get close enough to hear their voices and see the expressions on their faces. I craved it—the intimacy, the honor, the warmth.

But then... the branch snapped.

I fell. And when I hit the ground, I woke up within the dream, flat on my back, paralyzed, terrified, exposed. I tried to scramble away like a wild animal, ashamed and afraid, but I couldn't move. I had been caught. The moment I feared was happening.

That's when the boy walked over to me.

He leaned down and asked gently, "Are you okay?"

I responded quickly, with embarrassment:

"I'm so sorry. I didn't mean to interfere or disturb your time with your father."

Without hesitation, he reached down, took my hand, and pulled me to my feet. I couldn't move—yet somehow, when he touched me, I stood. Strength returned where there was none.

Then he turned me toward his father and said something I'll never forget:

"Father, this is one who wants to be part of our family. He was lost, but now he's found."

The father stepped forward, looked me in the face with compassion, and said:

"Welcome to our family. The things you see in My Son, you do—because everything My Son does pleases Me. And you'll always please Me if you do what He does."

Then the three of us—Father, Son, and me—walked off together through the clearing. And the dream ended. I never had it again.

God was using this dream to establish my confidence in sonship. Fatherlessness was healed. Belonging was restored. Intimacy increased, and calling God, Abba, became increasingly natural.

Belovedness Makes Consecration Joyful

We consecrate ourselves not to earn love, but because we are already loved.

The cry of "Abba, Father" is not weakness—it is sonship. Consecration is not restriction; it is a relationship. When we know God as Abba, surrender becomes joy, obedience becomes worship, and holiness becomes the natural expression of shared life.

You are not abandoned.

You are not tolerated.

You are home.

From Intimacy to Lordship

As affection deepens, lordship follows naturally.

Jesus is revealed not only as Savior, but as King—and we submit to Him not out of fear, but love. Intimacy and authority grow together. The more He is Lord in our secret places, the more power flows through our public lives.

This is an inside-out transformation—the kind the world has never seen but desperately needs.

Reflection Questions

1. What area of your life is the Holy Spirit gently inviting you to open?
2. Do you approach God more as a servant or as a son or daughter?
3. Where has affection toward God begun to awaken in you?

4. Are there still inner rooms that need to be yielded in trust?
   "Behold, I stand at the door and knock..." (Revelation 3:20)

Declaration

- I am no longer a slave to fear.
- I have been adopted into the family of God.
- The Spirit of Jesus lives in me and cries, "Abba, Father."
- My body is His temple, my heart His altar.
- I live from the inside out—consecrated, beloved, and aligned.

Chapter 8: The Deep Work

"Search me, O God, and know my heart; Try me, and know my anxieties; And see if there is any wicked way in me, And lead me in the way everlasting." —Psalm 139:23–24 (NKJV)

There comes a point in every believer's journey when the Holy Spirit knocks—not on the door of the heart to enter, but on the hidden doors within the heart, asking for deeper access.

These are not moments of first surrender, but of full surrender.

These are the rooms we sealed off—sometimes in pain, sometimes in pride, often in fear. This is where the deep work begins.

God is not satisfied with surface transformation. He is not interested in behavioral modification or spiritual performance. He desires transformation from the inside out. And that means He lovingly goes deeper than comfort allows.

The Spirit Who Knows All Things

When we gave our lives to Jesus, we received not only forgiveness, but a resident Helper—the Holy Spirit. He is not passive. He is wise, gentle, and intentional. He searches the depths of the soul, revealing what is hidden—not to condemn, but to heal.

Often, we resist this work. We want victory without vulnerability. We want anointing without pruning. Yet we can only rise as high as our roots grow deep.

If the roots are wounded, twisted, or planted in poor soil, the fruit will always be limited. The Holy Spirit patiently exposes unhealthy soil—wounded motives, fear-based thinking, pride, shame—not to shame us, but to replant us in truth and love. When roots are healed and anchored, they can sustain both godly character and the weight of future assignments.

"He restores my soul..." (Psalm 23:3)

Soul restoration is rarely instant. The soul - our mind, will and emotions, the real us, the eternal us - is where wounds and warped thinking reside. But the Spirit is patient, and His goal is wholeness.

From Fragrance to Fire

The holiness revealed through intimacy now deepens through refinement. What began as fragrance becomes purifying fire. The same Spirit who filled us for belonging now burns away what distorts God's likeness.

When the Spirit places His finger on an unhealed memory, a guarded motive, or a buried fear, He is not condemning—He is consecrating. Each surrendered place becomes an altar where His fire falls, consuming impurity and releasing deeper freedom.

This is the progressive sanctification of the Divine Genome—God's own nature unfolding through willing cooperation. As inner doors open, His Presence and glory expand in the temple. We are becoming a holy occupation.

Holiness moves from identity to influence. Presence matures into power.

When the Surgeon Arrives

To do deep work, the Spirit often begins at a sensitive place. Like a skilled surgeon, He says, "Let me in here." His intention is not harm, but healing. His scalpel is His Word.

"For the word of God is living and powerful... piercing even to the division of soul and spirit... and discerning the thoughts and intents of the heart." — Hebrews 4:12

This cutting is precise and purposeful. It separates truth from lies, light from darkness, old identity from new creation. This is not cosmetic adjustment—it is inner reformation.

During a particularly formative season of my life—just before stepping into Bible school and destiny training—the Holy Spirit began doing deep work in me through a series of recurring dreams. They were not dramatic spectacles. They were surgical.

Every dream was recurring, and over the years I've come to understand that in my younger years I was a little hard headed I guess, and it took repetition to get my attention.

He was not addressing my gifting.

He was addressing my foundation.

A Dream of Deliverance: Turning to Face the Enemy

For several nights in a row, I found myself running for my life in a dream. I would wake up exhausted, carrying the emotional residue of fear into the next day. I didn't even know who I was running from—but the urgency felt real.

Finally, one night in the dream, I cried out to God:

"Why am I running for my life? Who am I running from? Who's trying to kill me?"

The Lord answered plainly:

"You're running from the devil."

That revelation shifted everything.

I realized I had authority in Christ. I had no reason to run from the devil. In the dream, with that revelation, I stopped running. I stood up straight. I turned to face the enemy.

That's when I noticed something unexpected: he looked careless, unstable—almost foolish. Laughing. Stumbling. Running partially with his eyes closed. His strategy had not been strength. It had been intimidation.

His entire plan was simple: keep me running.

But the moment I stopped and turned to face him, he froze. When he realized I was no longer agreeing with fear, he turned—and ran from me.

"Submit to God. Resist the devil and he will flee from you."

—James 4:7

The dream exposed a hidden agreement with fear. Outwardly I was pursuing God. Inwardly I was still operating from survival.

God delivered me—not just from the enemy, but from the lie that I was vulnerable and hunted. He restored authority in my thinking. That internal shift prepared me to help others break free from fear as well.

When the Roof Falls: Deliverance from Self-Reliance

Around the same season, another recurring dream began.

In it, the roof of my house was collapsing. I scrambled frantically, trying to hold it up with whatever I could find. But the "props" I used were revealing: my ministry roles, my accomplishments, my spiritual titles.

"I'm a worship leader," I would say, propping one section.

"I lead Bible studies," to hold up another.

"I preach the Word," for the next.

Yet, no matter what I did, the roof kept falling.

In desperation, I finally cried out to God:

"Don't You care that my life is falling apart?"

And He answered—not harshly, but firmly—with a loud whisper:

"Let it fall."

In that moment, I understood. The structure I was trying to sustain was built partly on performance. Even my spiritual achievements had quietly become props—attempts to secure identity and stability through usefulness.

The dream also revealed a hidden stronghold: spiritual pride disguised as spiritual responsibility.

God was not destroying my calling.

He was dismantling self-reliance.

Deliverance came when I allowed the roof to fall and trusted Him to rebuild my life on something stronger than gifting—on surrender.

The Battlefield Revealed

These dreams were not random. They were the Holy Spirit performing heart surgery beneath the surface.

One exposed fear-driven survival.

The other exposed performance-driven identity.

The battlefield was not external.

It was internal.

And once those hidden agreements were confronted, the renewal of the mind could truly begin.

The Battlefield of the Mind

Much of the deep work occurs in the mind, because thoughts shape identity. The enemy cannot change our spiritual DNA, but he can influence our thinking if left unchecked.

"Be transformed by the renewing of your mind..." (Romans 12:2)

This renewal is not positive thinking—it is truthful thinking. When our thoughts agree with God, transformation follows. When they remain governed by fear, shame, or unbelief, the flow of divine life is restricted.

The Stage Manager Is on Duty

Early in my walk with the Lord, I struggled, as many do, with a flood of negative thoughts, lies from the enemy, and old mindsets that didn't match the new identity I had received in Christ. I was trying to obey what I was learning in the Word.

"...casting down arguments and every high thing that exalts itself against the knowledge of God, bringing every thought into captivity to the obedience of Christ." (2 Corinthians 10:5 NKJV)

But it felt overwhelming. Thoughts would come so fast, some subtle, some loud, and I didn't know how to "catch" them in real time. This caused me to struggle with guilt and shame over what was going on in the privacy of my mind.

Then something clicked. I had studied voice in college and had been part of several stage productions. In that world, I learned something critical: before any actor steps onto the stage, there's someone just offstage, usually called a stage manager or stage mom, whose job is to make sure the performer is ready before entering the stage.

They check the actor's costume, their props, and sometimes even their opening lines. And if that actor isn't prepared or appropriate for their entrance onto the stage, they feverishly try to get them ready to go on. The stage manager simply says, "Stop. You're not ready."

In answer to prayer for wisdom to overcome my thought life, the Lord helped me realize that my mind is like a stage, and thoughts are the actors waiting in the wings. Some thoughts are ready and true. Others are completely inappropriate, dressed in lies, fear, shame, or pride.

And it's my responsibility, by the Holy Spirit, to stand at the edge of that mental stage and decide:

Does this thought belong here?

Should I let it take center stage?

Would this please the One in the audience - God Himself?

I had to be the regular stagehand on duty to protect what goes onto the stage of my mind. That became my personal breakthrough. When a thought tries to enter, especially in stressful or vulnerable moments, I've learned to pause, examine it, and decide:

Is this in obedience to Christ?

Does this thought align with God's truth, God's character, and God's promises?

Would I want this playing in full view with God watching?

If not, I tell it: "You're not coming on." I reject it. I replace it with thoughts acceptable to God. And I invite the Holy Spirit to remind me of what should be center stage.

That illustration has helped me over and over again, and I've used it many times in discipleship to help others who struggle with overwhelming or deceitful thoughts. The goal isn't to suppress every bad thought with fear. It's to train ourselves to know what pleases God and to let only those things take the spotlight of our mind.

Marcus Norona, one of my business mentors, say's in regards to getting rid of all stinkin' thinkin',

"Flush the toilet before anybody has to see that mess!"

We are responsible for adjusting our attitude and speaking words wherever we are. The goal is not to fear thoughts, but to discern them. By the Holy Spirit, we learn what belongs on the stage of our mind—and what does not.

Dismantling Lies, Planting Truth

Behind every stronghold is a lie believed. The Spirit exposes lies not to humiliate us, but to uproot them. What is renounced is replaced with truth. Where lies once governed, altars of truth are raised. This is spiritual therapy from the inside out.

Healing the Soul: The Work of Sozo

Salvation is instant. Restoration is progressive The New Testament word sozo means to save, heal, deliver, and make whole. The cross purchased more than forgiveness—it purchased complete restoration of spirit, soul, and body. We were saved. We are being saved. We will be saved.

This is your Divine Genome unfolding through time until God's nature fully governs the soul.

Tears, Trust, and Transformation

The deepest work is often quiet. It happens in stillness, in tears, in the secret place. Yet it is here that freedom is forged and authority is gained.

"He who began a good work in you will complete it..." (Philippians 1:6)

God is not in a hurry. He is faithful.

Letting Go to Grow

Spiritual maturity is measured not by time, but by surrender. The deep work invites us to release what once protected us but now limits us. This work is not to be feared. It is to be treasured.

The deep work is God's invitation to partner with Him in the restoration of your soul, the renewing of your mind, and the activation of your spiritual DNA. It is not something to fear; it is something to treasure.

Reflection Questions

1. In what areas of your life have you been "running" instead of standing in your authority in Christ?
2. Are there fears that still influence your decisions, even though you know the truth of God's Word?
3. Have you been trying to "hold up the roof" of your life through performance, gifting, or spiritual activity?
4. Where might pride be disguised as responsibility or usefulness?
5. What would it look like to let God rebuild an area you have been trying to sustain in your own strength?
6. Is the Holy Spirit inviting you to grow in greater authority, deeper humility—or both?

Revised Declarations

- I stand in the authority given to me in Christ.
- I will no longer run from fear or intimidation.

- I submit to God and resist the devil, and he must flee.
- I release every false identity built on performance.
- I let go of self-reliance and receive God's sufficiency.
- I choose humility without insecurity and authority without pride.
- The Holy Spirit is strengthening my foundation.
- I welcome the deep work of inner transformation.
- God is rebuilding my life on truth, surrender, and grace.

Chapter 9: Setting Captives Free, From the Inside Out

Discernment, Authority, and the Flow of Indwelling Life

Freedom is never accidental.

It is revealed—then enforced.

Jesus did not set people free by reacting to symptoms.

He addressed the roots.

And He did so from union with the Father, not spiritual technique.

The same Spirit who lived and ministered through Jesus now lives within you.

Discernment: Seeing What God Sees

Discernment is not suspicion.

It is Spirit-given clarity.

"The manifestation of the Spirit is given to each one for the profit of all... to another discerning of spirits."

—1 Corinthians 12:7, 10 (NKJV)

Discernment enables us to perceive what is truly at work beneath the surface, so healing, freedom, and restoration can begin.

Through discernment, the Holy Spirit helps us distinguish:

- Between the voice of God, the voice of the flesh, and the voice of the enemy
- Between emotional wounds and spiritual strongholds
- Between behavioral symptoms and spiritual roots

Discernment does not accuse.

It reveals what God wants to heal.

Jesus: The Pattern of Discernment in Action

Jesus did not minister from methods.

He ministered from union.

Because He lived in constant communion with the Father, discernment flowed naturally through Him:

- He discerned Satan speaking through Peter's words "Get behind Me, Satan!" —Matthew 16:23
- He perceived the unspoken thoughts of religious leaders
  (Matthew 9:4; Luke 5:22)

- He recognized a spirit of infirmity behind physical limitation
  "Woman, you are loosed from your infirmity." — Luke 13:11–13
- He confronted demonic powers with calm authority (Mark 1:23–27)

Jesus did not react emotionally.

He responded spiritually.

His authority flowed from who He was united with, not from how loudly He spoke.

Authority Flows from Intimacy

Deliverance is not about volume.

It is about identity.

Jesus said:

"As the Father has sent Me, I also send you." — John 20:21

Authority is not something we work up.

It is something we carry because of who dwells within us.

When we live from the inside out:

- We don't strive to defeat darkness
- We enforce a victory already won

The enemy is not impressed by formulas.

He recognizes Christ in you.

The Gifts of the Spirit: Expressions of Indwelling Life

The gifts of the Spirit were never meant to replace communion.

They are meant to express it.

"Earnestly desire the best gifts..." —1 Corinthians 12:31

This is not ambition.

It is love made visible.

Manifestation Gifts (1 Corinthians 12:7–11)

Supernatural expressions of the Holy Spirit given as needed, for the freedom of others:

- Word of Wisdom — Insight into what to do or say in a specific moment
- Word of Knowledge — Revelation of facts known only by God
- Faith — A Spirit-given confidence to believe God without wavering
- Gifts of Healings — God's power restoring body, soul, or mind
- Working of Miracles — Divine intervention beyond natural law

- Prophecy — Speaking God's heart to build, encourage, or align
- Discerning of Spirits — Perceiving the spiritual source at work
- Different Kinds of Tongues — Spirit-inspired utterance
- Interpretation of Tongues — Spirit-given understanding

These gifts are not badges of maturity.

They are tools of love.

Discerning the Source: Flesh, Wound, or Spirit

Not every struggle is demonic.

Not every problem is psychological.

Discernment helps us recognize:

- When truth is needed
- When healing is needed
- When deliverance is needed

Without discernment, we may:

- Rebuke wounds that need healing
- Counsel spirits that need casting out
- Or tolerate lies that need truth

The Holy Spirit brings precision, not confusion.

Self-Deliverance and Daily Authority

Freedom does not depend on a prayer line.

Because the Spirit of God lives in you, authority begins at home.

Jesus said:

"If the Son makes you free, you shall be free indeed." —John 8:36

There are moments when we must speak truth boldly:

"Submit to God. Resist the devil, and he will flee from you." —James 4:7

You may declare:

"In the name of Jesus, I renounce every lie, every influence, and every work of darkness.

God is in His holy temple—I am it.

I belong to the Lord."

Deliverance that begins inside is deliverance that lasts.

Keeping the Temple Aligned

Jesus warned of an "empty house" (Matthew 12:43–45).

Freedom must be filled with Presence.

We remain free by:

- Abiding in Christ
- Renewing the mind
- Staying anchored in truth
- Living in daily communion with the Indwelling Godhead

Deliverance is not an event.

It is a way of living.

Final Charge: You Were Born to Set Captives Free

You may not feel like a deliverer.

But the Deliverer lives in you.

"The Spirit of the Lord is upon Me..." —Luke 4:18

Freedom flows where union is honored.

Chapter Summary

- Discernment reveals what God is ready to heal or remove
- Authority flows from intimacy, not effort
- The gifts of the Spirit are tools of love, not spiritual status
- Freedom begins inside and overflows outward

Reflection Questions

- Where have you sensed the Holy Spirit giving insight beneath the surface?
- Do you respond more from reaction or from union?
- What gift of the Spirit do you sense stirring within you for others' freedom?

Declaration

- live from union, not technique.
- I walk in discernment, love, and authority.
- The Spirit of God works through me to set captives free.
- Christ in me is greater than anything I face.

Chapter 10: Deliverance Through Discernment, Freedom by Revelation

As we continue our journey of living from the inside out, we inevitably encounter the reality of spiritual opposition. Scripture is clear: We wrestle not against flesh and blood but against principalities, powers, and spiritual forces of darkness (Ephesians 6:12). Many struggles that appear emotional, relational, or even circumstantial often have spiritual roots. What manifests outwardly is frequently driven inwardly.

The Holy Spirit within us is not only our Comforter; He is also our Revealer and Deliverer. He exposes what does not belong so that freedom can be restored and preserved.

As freedom increases, our capacity to commune with the indwelling God expands, allowing His authority to flow more fully through us to accomplish the works He desires to do with greater power.

The Gift of Discernment

Discernment of spirits is a spiritual gift (1 Corinthians 12:10) that enables us to distinguish between what is of God, what is of the human soul, and what is of the enemy. Through this gift, the Holy Spirit gives insight into unseen realities, helping us recognize when bondage is spiritual in nature rather than merely natural.

This kind of discernment is essential in deliverance ministry. We cannot effectively confront what we cannot see. But when God reveals the root cause, He also provides the solution. Discernment is not about fear or suspicion; it is about clarity. And clarity leads to freedom.

In the previous chapter, we learned that freedom begins from the inside out. Here, we discover that discernment helps guard that freedom by exposing the enemy's subtle attempts to return and reestablish influence.

Deliverance by Revelation

Many people remain trapped in cycles of defeat because they attempt to solve spiritual problems with natural solutions alone. While counsel, discipline, and wisdom have their place, spiritual bondage requires spiritual illumination. When the Holy Spirit reveals a lie, a wound, or a demonic influence, and we respond in agreement with truth, chains are broken. Jesus said, "You shall know the truth, and the truth shall make you free" (John 8:32).

Deliverance does not always appear dramatic. Sometimes it occurs quietly through repentance, surrender, and the renouncing of a lie. Other times it involves a bold declaration made in the authority of Jesus' name. Either way, the result is the same: freedom.

Every revelation that brings freedom also restores clarity—clarity about who we are, whose we are, and what we are called to carry.

Edith's Story: A Testimony of Reconciliation and Freedom

I first came to know Edith as she regularly combed through the recycling bins near our church and parsonage. She had attended our services a few times and was always kind and approachable. A gentleman nearby appeared to watch over her as she gathered cans and bottles, making sure she was safe.

Over time, I noticed that Edith had developed a pronounced limp. Something had happened—perhaps a stroke—that caused her to lift her foot and swing it forward with each step. Watching her struggle stirred compassion in my heart, and I felt a growing desire to help her in some way.

I began praying, asking God for discernment—how and when I might pray for her, and for His anointing to heal. I finally approached Edith and told her that God had placed her on my heart and that I wanted to pray for her healing. She smiled and said, "Sure—how about right now?"

She sat down on the curb while I stood in the street and began to pray. I asked God to manifest His presence and reveal Himself to her in a way she could not deny, drawing her into renewed fellowship with Him. Then I prayed for healing, commanding her foot to function as it was designed and for the muscles to relax and align.

As I continued praying, I noticed Edith's head was down, her face buried between her knees. Unsure of what was happening, I gently asked, "Edith, are you okay?" She looked up, tears streaming down her face, and with a radiant smile said, "We're talking again. We're talking! Thank you so much for praying for me—we're talking again!"

In that moment, I realized that the deepest healing God intended was not physical, but relational. He had restored one of His daughters to intimate fellowship with Himself. That was the miracle she needed most at that time.

Her healing began when heaven revealed the true root, even if I was clueless what He was doing. Heaven's revelation always produces restoration.

Walking in Authority

Once revelation exposes the enemy, authority enforces the victory.

Jesus gave authority to His followers to cast out demons and break spiritual strongholds (Mark 16:17). That authority was not reserved for a select few; it is given to all who believe. Yet authority flows from intimacy. We do not wield it like a tool; we carry it as an anointing, as representatives of Christ.

Deliverance is not about shouting louder or using special phrases. It is about knowing who you are in Christ, knowing who Jesus is in you, remembering that it is God doing the work through you, and standing firm in the truth that sets people free. The enemy is already defeated; we simply enforce that victory.

Self-Deliverance and Daily Authority

While there is great value in receiving prayer from others, there is also a place for daily self-deliverance—taking responsibility and authority over your own life as a child of God. You do not need to wait for a church service or a minister to speak freedom over you. Through Jesus, you have been given access, authority, and anointing for victory.

"But you have an anointing from the Holy One, and you know all things." -1 John 2:20 NKJV

It is wise to regularly declare who you are in Christ, cut off any fleshly or worldly influence that does not belong, renew your mind with truth, and proclaim the covering of Jesus' blood over your life.

You might pray something like this:

"In the name of Jesus, I command every evil influence to flee. I cut every cord of darkness. I plead the blood of Jesus over my mind, emotions, and body. I bring every thought into obedience to Christ. I declare: God is in His holy temple—I am it! Get behind me, Satan! I am a child of God, a minister of the gospel, and a soldier of the cross of Jesus Christ."

Such declarations reinforce an important truth: the temple of God is not a place; it is a person. And when the enemy comes knocking, he encounters a holy boundary, a surrendered vessel, and a life filled with God's Spirit.

Keeping the Temple Clean

After deliverance, it is essential to fill what has been cleared with God's Word, His presence, and His truth. Jesus warned that unclean spirits may return to an "empty house" (Matthew 12:43–45). Freedom must be followed by discipleship, worship, and daily intimacy with God.

Deliverance is not a one-time event; it is a lifestyle of staying free and helping others get free. As temples of the Holy Spirit, we carry His light into dark places—not only for ourselves, but for others.

Putting On the Armor of God Daily

Paul reminds us to "put on the whole armor of God" (Ephesians 6:10–18) so that we can stand against the schemes of the devil. Deliverance and discernment are sustained when we live clothed in Christ each day. The armor of God is not ritual; it is revelation, a warrior's declared authority.

- Belt of Truth – Keep your mind anchored in God's Word; truth holds everything together.
- Breastplate of Righteousness – Guard your heart from guilt and condemnation.
- Shoes of Peace – Walk in reconciliation, not reaction; carry peace wherever you go.
- Shield of Faith – Quench fiery doubts and accusations with unwavering trust in God.
- Helmet of Salvation – Protect your thoughts and identity as one redeemed and secure.
- Sword of the Spirit – Speak God's Word with authority and love; His truth cuts through deception.

When we put on the armor of God, we are not just preparing to fight for victory; we are standing in victory, fully covered by Christ's triumph. Each piece of armor reminds us that freedom is maintained through abiding, not striving. To live armored is to live aware of who He is in us and who we are in Him.

Declarations of Truth

- The Holy Spirit gives me discernment and revelation to walk in freedom.
- In Jesus' name, I have authority over every stronghold and lie of the enemy.
- I am clothed in the armor of God and stand firm in His victory.
- I am a carrier of God's presence, bringing light into every place of darkness.

Reflection Questions

1. Have you ever sensed a spiritual root behind a recurring struggle? What did the Holy Spirit reveal to you?
2. Are there lies you have believed that need to be replaced with God's truth?
3. Who in your life might be in bondage and need prayerful discernment or encouragement?

Chapter 11: Calling Forth Destiny - Prophetic Activation and Commissioning

The awakening of spiritual gifts and calling does not begin with position, title, or activity. It begins with restored life.

The human spirit was disconnected from divine life. God's image remained, but likeness and communion were disrupted. The flow of divine life was broken, not the design itself. Through Christ, communion is restored. And through the indwelling Holy Spirit, the Divine Genome—always present—can once again express the life, nature, and purposes of God from within the believer.

The Divine Genome was there all along, present from the moment of our creation, running parallel to our biological DNA. It was not added at salvation; it was awakened. What sin severed was not existence, but communion. Salvation restores that connection, allowing divine life to flow once again toward God from within the human spirit.

Jesus said, "Out of his innermost being will flow rivers of living water" (John 7:38, NASB). John explains that He was speaking of the Holy Spirit (v.

39). The word Jesus used for innermost being is the Greek 'koilia'—translated as belly (KJV), heart (NKJV), or that deepest inner place (NASB). It points to the dwelling place of God within the believer. This indwelling Presence is what makes spiritual communion, understanding, discernment, and activation possible. Jesus said the Holy Spirit flows from within us.

Because God lives within us, we are able to believe the Scriptures, recognize His voice, discern His gifts, and respond to His calling. Destiny does not originate in external roles or ministry titles; it unfolds from the koilia, where the Father, Son, and Holy Spirit dwell. What God encoded before time now begins to flow outward from within us, expressing His likeness, activating His gifts, and unfolding our calling and commission.

I believe it is possible that God designed our biological DNA and our spiritual DNA to run in parallel—one visible, one invisible—both present from the beginning, though the spiritual lay dormant toward God until awakened by the Holy Spirit. Just as biological DNA requires the proper environment to express its traits, the Divine Genome requires restored communion and divine indwelling to express God's purposes in and through us.

From this restored life within, calling is awakened, gifts are activated, and believers are prepared to step into destiny—not striving from the outside in, but flowing from the inside out.

Fivefold Ministry and the Spiritual Genome

The fivefold ministry gifts of Christ—Apostle, Prophet, Evangelist, Pastor, and Teacher—are not merely ministry positions, but expressions of Christ's own nature given to form His Body (Ephesians 4:11–13). These graces do not replace the inner work of God; they serve it, shaping and maturing what the Spirit is already releasing from within the believer.

Jesus Himself is the full expression of the Divine Genome. Through the fivefold, He continues His own ministry in His people—training, equipping, and preparing them to walk in love, truth, power, and maturity. These gifts are not marks of superiority, but functions of formation, designed to help believers grow into Christlikeness and effective service.

Below is a visual chart associating fivefold ministry expressions with spiritual DNA structure and function:

Nature of Christ	Fivefold Ministry	Spiritual Function
Jesus the Sent One	Apostle	Foundation Layer – Sent to Ground, Govern, and Guide
Jesus, the Voice of God	Prophet	Revelation Layer – Hear, See, Speak God's Heart
Jesus the Proclaimer	Evangelist	Outreach Layer – Preach, Draw, Gather to Christ
Jesus the Shepherd	Pastor	Nurture Layer – Care, Guard, Feed, Heal
Jesus the Truth	Teacher	Ground Layer – Explain, Illuminate, Impart Understanding

We are not called to admire these gifts from afar; we are meant to be formed by them from within as they are ministered in our midst. This is part of our activated spiritual DNA, developing us into likeness, maturity, and ultimately "the measure of the stature of the fullness of Christ" (Ephesians 4:12–13).

A Prophetic Parallel: Spiritual Genome and Biological Design

Biological DNA consists of four base pairs:

- Adenine (A)
- Thymine (T)
- Cytosine (C)
- Guanine (G)

These always pair as follows:

- Adenine (A) with Thymine (T)
- Cytosine (C) with Guanine (G)

These base pairs are the building blocks of life, holding together the genetic code that gives instructions and identity to our physical development.

As noted earlier, I believe it is possible that our biological DNA and our spiritual DNA run in parallel through our being. The following chart illustrates how these structures may symbolically correlate:

DNA BASE	NATURAL FUNCTION	FIVEFOLD GIFT	SPIRITUAL FUNCTION
Adenine (A)	Initiates structure; foundational base	Apostle	Lays spiritual foundations, governs, and sends
Thymine (T)	Pairs with Adenine to stabilize replication and ensure accuracy	Teacher	Grounds the Church in truth and understanding
Cytosine (C)	Repairs and protects; nurtures structure	Pastor	Cares for and protects the flock, encourages wholeness
Guanine (G)	Involved in signaling and energy transfer	Prophet	Declares God's word, offers vision and direction

But where does the Evangelist fit?

Though not one of the nucleotide bases, the Evangelist can be prophetically pictured as the sugar-phosphate backbone of the DNA strand:

- It binds everything together and enables communication along the chain.
- Evangelists proclaim the Good News, connecting heaven and earth.
- They join the other four giftings, carrying the message across the entire Body.

In this way, the Evangelist functions as a divine connector, holding the structure together and delivering life through the Gospel of Salvation and the Kingdom of God.

While this comparison is illustrative rather than doctrinal, it provides a helpful picture of God's ordered, intentional, and cooperative design. No strand exists for itself alone. Life is expressed best when everything is aligned and connected. In the same way, destiny is not fulfilled in isolation—it unfolds in the context God designed: the Body of Christ.

Prophetic Revelation: Calling Forth Destiny

The term prophetic may sound lofty, but at its core it simply means hearing from God and speaking what He says. In the context of destiny, prophetic words often reveal, confirm, or awaken what God intends to do in and through a person.

At times, God speaks directly to our hearts through dreams, desires, or guidance. At other times, He speaks through another believer with a word that resonates deeply. Throughout Scripture, this pattern is clear:

- David was anointed by Samuel long before he wore a crown (1 Samuel 16:12–13).
- Saul, later Paul, was commissioned through Ananias as God's chosen vessel at his conversion (Acts 9:15).
- Timothy was exhorted to stir up what had been spoken over him through prophecy (1 Timothy 1:18).

Prophecy does not create destiny; it calls it forth.

Often, a prophetic word resonates because it aligns with something already stirring in the heart. It brings clarity, courage, and direction. When tested and confirmed by Scripture and character, such words become markers along the journey, reminding us of God's intent as we walk it out in obedience.

Positioned for Function: Life in the Body

Every believer is placed in the Body of Christ with purpose. As the Spirit calls us into destiny, He positions us not only for identity, but for function.

"From whom the whole body, joined and knit together by what *every joint supplies*... causes growth of the body for the edifying of itself in love" (Ephesians 4:16, NKJV).

Prophetic activation often clarifies gifts and awakens purpose, helping us recognize where we are meant to serve. As those gifts come alive, we grow into our God-assigned role through interaction with others—functioning as healthy joints that both supply and receive life.

Destiny is personal, but it is never private.

Commissioning: Stepping Into What God Has Called Forth

Receiving revelation is one thing; stepping into obedience is another. Commissioning is the moment when calling moves from understanding to action.

From the beginning, God commissioned humanity: "Let Us make man in Our image... let them have dominion" (Genesis 1:26). Jesus restored that commission. Before His resurrection, He sent the disciples to preach and heal. After His resurrection, He breathed on them and said, "Receive the Holy Spirit" (John 20:22). Then He declared, "All authority has been given to Me... Go therefore" (Matthew 28:18–20).

Commissioning always flows from impartation. The Holy Spirit empowers what He initiates. Sometimes commissioning happens publicly through prayer and laying on of hands; other times it happens quietly in the heart with a simple but costly, "yes."

Destiny is not fulfilled in a day—it is entered decisively and fulfilled progressively.

Destiny Unfolded in Community

Calling matures in relationship. Gifts are refined through service. Love is perfected in community. When each believer functions in their grace, Christ is revealed more clearly through His Body.

Acts 13:1–3 shows this pattern at Antioch, where Barnabas and Saul were already serving when the Holy Spirit spoke and the church commissioned them. The calling was already present; activation came through recognition and release.

God is as invested in the process as He is in the destination. Often there is a season between prophetic promise and fulfillment. During that time, the Holy Spirit shapes character, deepens humility, and prepares the vessel.

Responding to the Call with Humility and Faith

How we respond to a prophetic word matters. Pride can rush ahead; unbelief can shrink back. Both can delay fulfillment. God invites partnership marked by humility, trust, and obedience.

"Do not despise prophecies. Test all things; hold fast what is good" (1 Thessalonians 5:20–21). Prophetic destiny is both a gift and a process.

Personal Story: A Fivefold Prophetic Activation

I will never forget the day God confirmed His call on my life through a powerful prophetic word. I had just begun serving as Senior Pastor at Calvary Church in San Pablo, California. One day, while attending a fellow Pastor's service in Oakland, a guest Prophet named Shirley Beaver was ministering. I slipped in quietly and sat near the back, not wanting to draw attention to myself.

As the meeting was coming to a close for lunch, the prophet appeared unsettled, as though she was not finished. Suddenly, she looked in my direction and began to prophesy. She said, "I see you're a worshiper. You love to worship God. I see you're an evangelist—you love to lead people to Jesus." Then she continued, "But you're also a pastor. You have a shepherd's heart, and you love to care for people."

She paused again and added, "You're also a teacher. You love the Word of God. You study deeply, even digging into the Greek and Hebrew." Then she paused once more and said, "The Lord says you're also a prophet, and you're an apostle. God is going to use you to open ministries and do many different things in the Kingdom."

By that point, tears were flowing freely. She did not know me, but God did. Through her, He was confirming what He had been forming in me over many years. I had been deeply involved in evangelism, served at Billy Graham Crusades, discipled others, and was now pastoring while growing in my love for Scripture and teaching. That prophetic word did not create something new; it affirmed what God had already been weaving together within me.

I was reminded of the Lord's voice years earlier, when He had spoken to me and said, "Get yourself in position to be a pastor, and I'll take it from there." Her word stretched my vision of my personal capacity. As I continued to walk in obedience, God opened doors I could never have planned. I was led to organize regional events such as March for Jesus,

Bay Area Skateboarding Competitions, and West County Evangelism Explosion outreaches. I became a police chaplain, a public school teacher, a college and high school assistant basketball coach, a city councilmember, served as mayor twice, and as President of the San Pablo Rotary Club.

With regional Intercessors, we hosted a large convocation of Christian First Nations People, including Grand Chief Lynda Prince and the 120 Drums, who came from all over the US and Canada, for an entire weekend to prepare the gateway for the Lytton Band of Pomo Indians. The Tribal Chief received Christ that weekend, and eventually the San Pablo City Council approved the land and agreement for the Tribe to establish their Reservation, and the first Casino in a California urban area.

Looking back, I can say with humility and gratitude that none of this came from striving for position. None of it was something I sought; for the most part, I was in over my head. I honestly didn't know people who did these kinds of things. All of it was a first for anyone in my biological family.

It unfolded through obedience, unselfish service, and God's grace to walk in my destiny. That prophetic moment helped me embrace the full measure of God's calling on my life—not as a title to wear, but as a responsibility to steward.

God used a prophetic word to confirm what He had been forming over time. It did not create the calling; it clarified it. That word became an anchor point along the journey, reminding me to stay positioned and faithful, and watch what the Lord will do.

Destiny Is Unfolded in Community

While calling is personal, its development happens in the Body. When each believer functions in their grace, the Body grows in love and maturity. Destiny is not competition; it is completion. And completion can't happen without us individually growing in the first and second greatest commandments:

Jesus said to him, 'You shall love the Lord your God with all your heart, with all your soul, and with all your mind. [38] This is the first and great commandment. [39] And the second is like it: You shall love your neighbor as yourself.'

These must be exercised with the members of the Body of Christ as we gather and worship and grow together. Then we learn to expand His love to others.

Be a Good Joint

"from whom the whole body, joined and knit together by what every joint supplies, according to the effective working by which every part does its share, causes growth of the body for the edifying of itself in love." (Ephesians 4:16 NKJV)

Every gathering creates new joints in the Body. Whoever you are next to becomes a point of connection where grace and love can flow.

Listen well. Pray simply. Encourage faithfully. Minister as the Spirit leads—not to fix, but to strengthen, encourage and comfort.

"He who prophesies speaks edification and exhortation and comfort to men" (1 Corinthians 14:3, NKJV).

The Developing Body and the Prepared Bride

This is the Body growing into likeness (Ephesians 4:15). And it is also the Bride being made ready (Revelation 19:7). When every joint supplies love and every member reflects Christ, the Church mirrors the beauty of her King.

Declarations of Truth

- God has uniquely designed me with gifts and purpose. My spiritual DNA carries the imprint of His calling.
- I receive and respond to prophetic words with humility, discernment, and faith.

- I am a joint in the Body of Christ, called to supply strength, wisdom, and encouragement.
- I am part of the Bride being prepared in love, clothed in righteousness, and radiant with His glory.

Reflection Questions

1. Have you ever received a prophetic word about your calling? How did you respond?
2. What gifts or passions has God placed in you that may point to your assignment?
3. How are you currently functioning as a "joint" in the Body, serving and encouraging others?
4. How might God be using your present placement to prepare you and others for Christ's return?

Final Note

When every strand of the Divine Genome connects in love, the Body becomes the Bride, and Jesus is fully seen in His people. This is the ultimate activation—not just destiny fulfilled, but love perfected.

Chapter 12: No Ceiling, You Were Born for More!

As we draw closer to the conclusion of this journey, it is important to recognize that we have not truly reached an end at all—only a new beginning. The journey of activating your Divine Genome is a lifelong adventure that continues until we see Jesus face to face. There is no ceiling to how much we can grow, how deeply we can know God, or how fully He can express Himself through us. Because God Himself lives within us, our potential in Him is truly limitless. You were born for more than what this world alone can offer; you were born to carry heaven's presence on earth.

Breaking Limitations

One of the enemy's consistent tactics is to impose false limitations on God's people—whispering that we are disqualified, powerless, or that we have somehow reached the maximum of what God will do in our lives. But God says otherwise.

"Now to Him who is able to do exceedingly abundantly above all that we ask or think, according to the power that works in us" (Ephesians 3:20, NKJV).

Pause and let that truth settle in. The power at work within you—the Holy Spirit—can accomplish far beyond your greatest prayers or imagination. Any ceiling pressing down on your life does not come from God. With Him, the horizon is always expanding.

Consider the journey we've explored throughout this book:

- In intimacy with God, there are always deeper levels of fellowship and revelation to discover.
- In transformation, there are more layers of our character to be refined.
- In intercession and spiritual authority, there are greater victories to be won and mountains to be moved by faith.
- In evangelism and prophetic ministry, there are more souls to reach and deeper ways the Spirit desires to speak to human hearts.
- In calling and destiny, God opens doors we never imagined and invites us into assignments crafted by His wisdom.

All these dimensions of Spirit-filled life share one truth: they are open-ended. There is no place where we can say, "I've had enough of God," or "I've seen all He can do." Church history proves that God delights in outdoing Himself in every generation, releasing fresh waves of His presence and power.

Why not through you—and through your generation?

"Most assuredly, I say to you, he who believes in Me, the works that I do he will do also; and greater works than these he will do" (John 14:12, NKJV).

Greater works. This is not spiritual exaggeration—it is Jesus' own promise to those who believe. We are not meant to shrink back, but to live with holy expectation.

Living with Holy Expectation

Living with the awareness that "I am God's holy temple" reshapes how we approach each day. It cultivates holy expectation. Instead of waking up thinking, "Just another day," we begin to say, "Lord, what are we doing today? Who might You touch? How might I grow?"

This does not mean every day will be filled with dramatic miracles or visible breakthroughs. But it does mean every day is significant, carrying divine possibility. The more we expect God and make room for Him, the more we recognize His hand at work.

We were never born merely to survive or succeed by worldly standards. We were born to glorify God as His sons and daughters, filled with His Spirit. There is a Kingdom to advance—in our families, workplaces, communities, and to the ends of the earth. Ultimately, the "more" we were born for is more of Him.

The apostle Paul, after decades of walking with Christ, still declared:

"That I may know Him and the power of His resurrection, and the fellowship of His sufferings" (Philippians 3:10, NKJV).

He pressed on, "forgetting those things which are behind and reaching forward to those things which are ahead" (Philippians 3:13, NKJV). If Paul saw no ceiling in knowing Christ, neither should we.

This posture guards us from complacency. We celebrate what God has already done, but we refuse to settle. There are always new facets of God's nature to encounter, new assignments to receive, and new expressions of His grace to experience—not for thrill-seeking, but as part of a growing relationship with Him.

Continuing the Journey

How do we continue forward in practical terms? We return to the foundations:

- Practice the Shut-In with the Godhead, develop personal communion, cultivate His Presence.

- Stay connected — Walk daily in fellowship with God through prayer, worship, and His Word.
- Stay yielded — Respond to the Holy Spirit's promptings with a willing heart.
- Stay in community — We are the Body of Christ and need one another.
- Keep learning — Remain a student of Jesus; seek mentors and heroes of faith who inspire you toward the "more."
- Dream with God — Embrace godly ambitions planted by His Spirit and take obedient steps as He leads.
- Cultivate gratitude — Regularly say, "I'm grateful, Lord." Gratitude aligns the heart with heaven.
- Expand by grace — Remember that "more" does not come through striving, but through growing from glory to glory as we behold Him.

The Final Commission: A Call to Divine Partnership

Throughout creation, countless beings serve the Almighty with perfect devotion. The twenty-four elders cast their crowns in worship. The four living creatures proclaim His holiness. Angels execute His commands with zeal.

Yet humanity stands uniquely positioned—created in God's image and likeness, entrusted with dominion, and called to reflect His nature on earth.

The Divine Genome is not a poetic metaphor; it is a spiritual reality. It speaks of God's indwelling presence, empowering us to live from the inside out and to fulfill His eternal purposes.

Scripture also warns that darkness will intensify. The dragon will empower the beast to wage war against the saints (Revelation 13:1–7), and allegiance will be demanded through deception and pressure (Revelation 13:16–17). In such times, our security will not rest in systems, but in the seal of the Holy Spirit.

The call remains clear: to walk in unwavering partnership with the Father, Son, and Holy Spirit.

Enduring Through Intimacy

As pressures increase and the world grows darker, intimacy with God will become our greatest safeguard. There may come times when access to church buildings, online resources, or even nearby believers is limited. But isolation will never mean abandonment.

Those who have cultivated friendship with the Father, communion with Jesus, and sensitivity to the Holy Spirit will stand unshaken. Christ in you, the hope of glory, will be the wellspring of strength, wisdom, and comfort.

Now is the time to build the inner life.

Learn to hear His voice in stillness, to draw upon His presence in solitude, and to live from the inside out when outward supports are stripped away. When the storm comes, it will be too late to build the ark—so build it now.

Heaven's Worship Is an Eternal Symphony

Heaven resounds with ceaseless praise. Angels, living creatures, and elders proclaim God's holiness without end. Yet redeemed humanity adds a song unknown to angels—the song of redemption. (Revelation 14:3 NKJV)

Angels marvel at the voices of those who were once lost and are now found. And still, the culmination awaits a future gathering, when the redeemed, clothed in glorified bodies, will stand before the throne and lift a new song—the Song of the Lamb. Angels serve the Throne, the Saints, the Bride of Christ, shares the Throne. (Revelation 3:21 NKJV)

Conclusion: No Ceiling, Only Glory

This book does not close a journey; it opens one. The Divine Genome is not a concept to admire—it is an invitation to become who you were created to be:

a carrier of God's nature, a reflection of His glory, and a participant in His eternal purpose.

You were never meant to live the Christian life from the outside in. You were created to live from the inside out—transformed by intimacy, empowered by grace, and led by the indwelling Godhead.

We have journeyed from identity to intimacy, from brokenness to restoration, from salvation to activation. We have named the dangers that hinder us and the remedy found in relationship with the Father, Son, and Holy Spirit.

And now, you stand at the threshold of what comes next. God is not finished with you. Heaven sees you. The Triune God delights in you. The host of heaven stands ready.

Final Words: A Personal Commission

So go.

Walk with God.

Let the Divine Genome be fully alive in you.

Let the fire burn in the temple.

Let your life become His voice, His hands, His glory in the earth.

Live from the inside out.

Speak what He speaks.

Move when He moves.

And always enjoy talking with Pappa, Jesus, and Holy Spirit.

They are in you and with you forever.

They are the marks of God upon you.

Connect His Throne on your heart with His Throne in Heaven.

Be Heaven's ambassador on the earth.

Heaven knows you.

The unseen realm knows who you are.

There is no limit to the intimacy you and God can share.

And as you go, remember this:

There is no ceiling over your life.

Only sky.

Only glory.

Chapter 13: The War on the Divine Genome

Why the Enemy Is Targeting Human DNA and the God-Conscious Soul

A Final War for the Blueprint

There is a war raging over the image and likeness of God in humanity. It is a conflict that began in the garden, unfolded throughout history, and has now entered its most dangerous phase—not merely through temptation or deception, but through an attempt to reprogram the very essence of what it means to be human.

The enemy is no longer satisfied with influencing behavior alone; he seeks to rewrite the design itself. Through advances in biotechnology, transhumanism, and identity confusion, Satan is waging an all-out assault on what this book has called the Divine Genome—God's spiritual blueprint within every person. This blueprint carries the capacity for intimacy with God, righteousness, creativity, spiritual authority, and moral conscience.

This chapter exposes why the enemy is determined to destroy that design—and why God's redemptive plan cannot be stopped.

The Enemy's Longstanding Pattern - Corrupt the Seed

"And I will put enmity between you and the woman, and between your seed and her Seed..." Genesis 3:15

From the beginning, Satan has waged war against the seed. He cannot create life, so he seeks to corrupt what God creates.

Many Biblical Scholars interpret Genesis 6 to reveal that fallen angels mated with human women, producing a hybrid race known as the Nephilim, defiling the human genetic line. The corruption became so severe that God intervened through the Flood to preserve humanity through Noah. Satan's objective then is the same now: to alter humanity so it can no longer fully carry the image and likeness of God.

Today, the assault no longer comes through angelic beings, but through technology, ideology, and identity manipulation—modern tools serving an ancient agenda.

Why DNA? Why Now?

DNA is not merely a biological molecule; it is a message. It carries the instructions that shape who we are physically, mentally, emotionally, and—by divine design—even spiritually. The human conscience, that inner awareness of God and moral accountability, is woven into this design.

Scripture affirms this truth:

"...who show the work of the law written in their hearts, their conscience also bearing witness..." Romans 2:15

Satan understands that if he can alter human DNA or deaden the conscience, he can sever the human soul from the pull of heaven. His ultimate strategy is to produce a godless humanity—people who no longer sense God's voice, no longer feel conviction, and are therefore primed to give allegiance to the beast system (Revelation 13:4, 16–17).

The Tools of Today: A Modern Tower of Babel

What we are witnessing in the modern world is not random innovation, but coordinated spiritual resistance against God's design.

1. Transhumanism — The attempt to merge humanity with artificial intelligence and machines, replacing dependence on God with synthetic evolution.
2. Genetic Editing — Technologies such as CRISPR enable the alteration of human traits, even before birth, with some openly proposing the removal of what they call "religious tendencies."
3. Gender and Identity Disruption — When foundational identity is dismantled, moral clarity and divine order collapse.
4. Mind Control and Media Saturation — Constant distraction, manipulation, and entertainment dull spiritual sensitivity and desensitize the conscience.

These are not merely cultural trends. They are spiritual strategies aimed at dismantling God's internal design.

God's Answer: The Restoration of the Divine Genome

"Therefore, if anyone is in Christ, he is a new creation..." 2 Corinthians 5:17

God has not left humanity vulnerable. Through the death and resurrection of Jesus Christ, a supernatural rebirth has been made possible—the reactivation and restoration of the Divine Genome.

When we are born again:

- We receive a new nature (2 Peter 1:4)
- God writes His law upon our hearts (Hebrews 8:10)
- Our conscience is cleansed and purified (Hebrews 9:14)
- The seed of God is implanted within us (1 John 3:9)

This is not symbolic language alone; it is the transformation of spiritual DNA. What sin corrupted, Christ restores from the inside out.

You Are the Countermove

You, believer, are God's countermove to the enemy's agenda. Your very existence—indwelled by the Father, Son, and Holy Spirit—stands as living proof that the Divine Genome cannot be erased.

You carry:

- The image of the Father
- The authority of the Son
- The power of the Holy Spirit

And this calling extends beyond you. You are commissioned to discern, awaken, and help restore others who are still operating under a dormant or corrupted spiritual code. You are a restorer of the breach, a carrier of heaven's DNA, and a witness to God's unalterable design.

Declarations

Speak these aloud:

- "I am fearfully and wonderfully made in the image of God."
- "I carry the Divine Genome—God's spiritual blueprint for identity, purpose, and power."
- "No technology, ideology, or deception can rewrite who God created me to be."
- "I am born again, sealed by the Holy Spirit, and made for intimacy with my Creator."

Reflection Questions

1. In what ways do you see the enemy targeting identity and conscience in today's world?

2. Have you ever sensed the Divine Genome within you being attacked, suppressed, or dormant? How did God begin restoring it?
3. How can you help others rediscover or activate their God-given spiritual identity?

Closing Charge

You were not born for compromise. You were born for consecration and conquest. As the enemy intensifies his final attempt to alter humanity, God is raising a people who know who they are, know Whose they are, and will not bow to a false image.

Let this chapter not be the end—but the call to your full activation.

Epilogue: From Activation to Destiny - Living from the Inside Out

You've made it to the end of this book, but in God's eyes, you've just stepped into the beginning of a whole new life.

You've read of Eden and the Fall, of the image and likeness planted within you, of Jesus restoring what was lost, and of the Holy Spirit now dwelling in your very being. You've seen how the Divine Genome was broken, but is now being restored in Christ. You've learned to yield to the Father, walk with Jesus, and host the Holy Spirit within your temple. You've been challenged to go deeper, love stronger, discern more clearly, and minister with courage.

But the goal has never been just learning. The goal has always been activation.

Now, the world is waiting for the unveiling of the sons and daughters of God (Romans 8:19). That means you.

This world doesn't need more performers. It needs presence-bearers. It needs people who live from the inside out, who refuse to be shaped by culture and instead carry the culture of heaven everywhere they go.

You Were Made for This Hour

You were born for such a time as this. You are not a mistake, not an accident, not a survivor of the chaos. You are a carrier of the Divine Genome, the spiritual DNA of the Creator, awakened through salvation and empowered by the Holy Spirit.

You have a calling.

You have spiritual authority.

You have access to the throne of grace and the voice of God.

And you are never alone.

He lives in you. He walks with you. And He wants to work through you.

Be Who You Are

Let the profound truths of this book transform your daily walk:

- Let prayer become dialogue.
- Let worship become overflow.
- Let obedience become joy.
- Let revelation become action.

You are now responsible for the light you've received. And you're equipped to carry it.

So, tear down every altar in your life that does not belong to Him.

Step into your identity with boldness.

Discern the times with clarity.

And awaken the image of God in others with love and authority.

Stewarding His Presence: A Word of Encouragement to Leaders

Before we can guide others into meaningful encounters with God's presence within, we must personally experience the value of being Shut-In with Him ourselves (see Chapter 6). This is where spiritual capacity is enlarged, sensitivity to the Holy Spirit is sharpened, and confidence in inner communion with God is formed.

Pastors and worship leaders have an extraordinary opportunity in this hour. For many years, they have faithfully led congregations into powerful encounters with God's presence, often emphasizing the truth of His indwelling presence and the Scriptures that reveal Him living within His temple—His people. Yet guiding teams and congregations into a conscious, shared experience of that indwelling reality can feel challenging.

This is where personally practicing the Shut-In exercise becomes so valuable. As leaders experience it firsthand, they gain language, discernment, and spiritual capacity to lead their worship teams into genuine encounters with God's indwelling presence from the inside out.

In turn, those teams are then able to guide congregations more effectively—not toward an external visitation, but into awareness and communion with the God who already dwells within them. As our collective capacity for God is enlarged from within, He is given greater freedom among us—to move as He desires, sovereign in His works, never summoned, always Present Lord.

As pastors and worship leaders steward this practice together with their teams, Shut-Ins become more than a devotional moment; they become a formative discipline that shapes how worship is carried publicly. Moments of stillness, surrender, and inner communion begin to shape the spiritual environment long before the congregation gathers. What is cultivated within the team becomes what can be facilitated among the people.

This is the Apostle Paul's prayer for the Church:

"...that He (Jesus) would grant you, according to the riches of His glory, to be strengthened with might through His Spirit *in the inner man.*"
(Ephesians 3:16 NKJV)

This strengthening of the inner man is the foundation of spiritual capacity. As leaders learn to steward this inner strengthening through communion with God, they are equipped to lead others—not toward a distant presence, but into conscious fellowship with the indwelling God.

I have seen vision of the focus and language of worship naturally begin to shift. Songs are no longer oriented toward calling for God to come down or from outside us, even into the room, but toward inviting what God has placed within to come forth. Living waters begin to flow from within the people of God (John 7:37-39), just as Jesus promised. The rivers flow from within the temple(s) (Ezekiel 47:1-12), increasingly, healing everything they touch. Worship language increasingly connects the congregation with the Father, the Son, and the Holy Spirit who dwell within them. Holiness, among other discipleship themes, is now naturally embraced.

This shift is reinforced as worship leaders intentionally sing Scriptural truth that declare God is dwelling within His people. As these truths are sung, faith is strengthened, awareness is awakened, and worship becomes a response to indwelling presence rather than a request for distant visitation. Habitation begins to be realized, recognized, and established.

In this way, worship becomes less about reaching for God and more about responding to Him. Leaders steward His presence faithfully—not by striving to create it, but by learning to recognize it, honor it, and lead others into it from the inside out.

For those who desire support in this journey, the author is available to facilitate Shut-In practice sessions for leaders and teams. In addition, training and certification are available for pastors and worship leaders who sense a call to steward this practice within their own churches or regions. These sessions are designed not to create dependence, but to equip leaders to guide others confidently into personal and corporate encounters with God's indwelling presence.

For congregations, ministries, or training cohorts, discounted pricing is available for bulk book orders. Leaders are welcome to contact the author directly for details on bulk sales and distribution within their church or network.

The Author is already preparing two follow-up companion books to complete the set.

Book 1

God is in His Holy Temple: Activating Your Divine Genome

Book 2

God is in His Holy Temple: Establishing a Holy Habitation

Book 3

Divine Genome Daily Activation: A 365 - Day Devotional

Final Declarations & Prayer of Activation

Let This Be Your Amen!

These declarations and this prayer are designed to awaken, align, and activate everything God has placed within you. Speak them aloud. Pray them in faith. Return to them often. This is your divine 'yes' to living from the inside out.

Declarations of Identity and Destiny

I declare:

- I am created in the image and likeness of God.
- I have been born again and carry the Divine Genome of my Creator.
- My body is a holy temple, and God Himself lives in me.
- I hear His voice, discern His leading, and walk in His power.
- No counterfeit code will redefine who I am; I belong to the Lord.
- I tear down every false altar in my life and surrender fully to Jesus.
- I am being transformed from glory to glory by the Spirit of the Lord.

- I am a carrier of His presence, a releaser of His truth, and a restorer of others.
- I will live from the inside out—for intimacy, obedience, and eternal purpose.
- I was born for such a time as this, and I will fulfill my Kingdom assignment.

Prayer of Activation

Father God,

Thank You for revealing Your heart, Your presence, and Your divine design to me through this book. I receive the truth that I am fearfully and wonderfully made—not only biologically, but spiritually—according to Your eternal purpose.

Jesus,

You are my Savior and my King. I thank You for restoring the Divine Genome through Your sacrifice and resurrection. I crown You, Lord, over every part of my being. I turn away from every false altar and align my heart fully with Yours.

Holy Spirit,

I invite You to fill every room of my temple. Awaken every dormant gift. Burn away every compromise. Activate my spiritual DNA so that I may walk in power, love, and truth. Teach me to live from the inside out—sensitive to Your voice, surrendered to Your will, and steadfast in my calling. Use me to set others free, to speak destiny, and to release Your presence on the earth.

I declare that from this day forward, I will walk in the fullness of who I am—in Christ, by the Spirit, for the glory of the Father.

God is in me, His holy temple, activating my divine genome for His glory and for my destiny as His Servant in this life!

In the mighty name of Jesus Christ my Lord—

Yeshua HaMashiach—

King of Kings and Lord of Lords,

Amen!

Benediction

"The Lord bless you and keep you;

The Lord make His face shine upon you,

And be gracious to you;

The Lord lift His countenance upon you,

And give you peace."

Numbers 6:24-26

May the presence of the Father walk with you.

May the voice of Jesus lead you.

May the fire of the Holy Spirit burn within you.

And may your life shout to the world:

"God is in His holy temple, let all the earth be silent before Him!"

Now go... and live from the inside out.

www.ingramcontent.com/pod-product-compliance
Lightning Source LLC
LaVergne TN
LVHW010927110826
845149LV00013B/2509

* 9 7 9 8 9 9 3 8 0 9 2 2 9 *